ATLANTA
RECORD STORES

AN ORAL HISTORY

CHAD RADFORD

THE
History
PRESS

Published by The History Press
Charleston, SC
www.historypress.com

First published 2023

Manufactured in the United States

ISBN 9781467142977

Library of Congress Control Number: 2022948298

Notice: The information in this book is true and complete to the best of our knowledge. It is offered without guarantee on the part of the author or The History Press. The author and The History Press disclaim all liability in connection with the use of this book.

CONTENTS

ACKNOWLEDGEMENTS

This book is dedicated to Laura Hunt, my loving partner, who for decades has watched me spend all of my money on records. She has accompanied me on long, out-of-the-way drives and train rides to find record stores everywhere from Paris, France, to Cedar Rapids, Iowa.

And to Milton Jones, one of the first people I met in Atlanta (working at Wax'n'Facts), who booked some of the greatest and most challenging music that I have ever encountered. Music that I may have never seen or heard otherwise. Atlanta has suffered since you left. RIP. And to Victoria Nicholson and the rest of the Euphonics Productions crew, too.

Hearty and exhaustive thanks are also due to Laura Hunt and Ana Balka for their keen eyes and copy-editing expertise; Mark Gunter from Fantasyland for answering so many of my late-night emails; and Sean Bourne for keeping me informed over the years. Also to Todd at Low Yo Yo Records in Athens, Kip Thomas at *Record Plug* magazine, Tom Cheshire, Frank Reiss and Loring Kemp at A Cappella Books, James Joyce, *Down For Life* magazine, Jessica Smith at *Flagpole*, Mary Monseur at the Smithsonian Institute, Randy Castello and Joe Gartrell at The History Press for his limitless patience. Thank you for bearing with me. And most importantly to Mike Howard and Andrea Butkiewicz Howard at Drastic Plastic for opening the door to this journey.

WELCOME TO ATLANTA

An idea came floating my way sometime around the fall of 2017: write a book about Atlanta record stores. It seems simple enough, at least upon initial approach and at least as an abstract concept. And what a great sound bite to throw around when people ask what I'm up to: "Well, I'm writing a book about Atlanta record stores!"

The possibilities are endless, but where does one start with such an endeavor? Put together a comprehensive list of every shop inside (and outside) the I-285 perimeter that has sold CDs, vinyl records and so on? That sounds like a punishing read, and it would take an entire lifetime to assemble.

Perhaps a more important question to ask is, Why write a book about Atlanta record stores?

The all-knowing, all-seeing algorithm knows that I've been doing some deep Google searches into Atlanta's record store past and into record stores in general. There is a common public perception that there are no more record stores left, but this is simply not true.

I get it. There aren't as many record stores as there once were, now that the general population looks to their phones for music, but there are more than enough people out there in the wild who still want and need to touch the music—and their numbers are growing again.

At the time of this writing (circa 2022), there are more than twenty record stores in and around the city of Atlanta. There are the big three: Wax'n'Facts, Wuxtry and Fantasyland, each of which is quickly approaching its fiftieth anniversary.

Philip Frobos of the Atlanta post-punk band OMNI searching the new arrivals crates at Wax'n'Facts in 2018. *Photo by Chad Radford.*

Criminal Records has the highest profile in town. The shop's owner, Eric Levin, is a co-founder of Record Store Day, the annual Hallmark holiday when people line up at mom-and-pop record shops to buy the limited edition releases du jour.

Across the street from Criminal, there is Moods Music. Since opening the shop in 2000, owner Darryl "D-Nice" Harris has kept a tight focus on soul (classic and neo), Afrobeat, rare funk, jazz, acid house and Latin music on people's turntables and in their ears—music that Harris has spent a lifetime pursuing and sharing.

The stage in the recently christened Soul Village next door to Moods brings a live music dimension to the space, pushing the yin and yang of the communal aspects of the traditional record store experience to a deeper and a higher level.

Beatlab lies tucked away behind and above Junkman's Daughter. Like Moods Music, Beatlab fosters an environment that's more than an outlet for DJ and producer gear while appealing to the city's graffiti writers and mural artists. If you need vinyl to spin, new needles, turntable maintenance, a mixer, a mic or spray paint caps for perfecting fine details and line work, BeatLab is the spot for serving all five elements of hip-hop: emceeing, deejaying, breakin', graff writing and beatboxing.

To most intowners, DBS Sounds Inc. is a remote Southside outpost. But for owner Derwin "Tobago" Benito, the shop is a labor of love that caters to the Riverdale community and is an essential stop on Atlanta's independent record store tour for new and classic urban music on vinyl.

The "DBS" in the shop's name stands for Tobago's family members' names: Derwin, Bridget, Shanae. Each year on Record Store Day, DBS hosts a mighty block party in the Riverdale Plaza Shopping Center, complete with cookouts, DJ sets and in-store appearances and record-signing sessions that have featured everyone from Killer Mike and Cee-Lo Green to Angie Stone of the Sequence and DJ Jelly.

In the Battery on the Northside, standing in the shadow of Truist Park where the Atlanta Braves play, Waterloo Sunset has reigned supreme for the last few years. As of press time, however, the shop's owner, Ted Ross, had recently vacated the Battery, with the promise of announcing a new location soon—not soon enough, though, for the 2023 pressing of the book you now hold in your hands.

In Decatur, one of the most recent shops to join in the mix, the Record Loft, has also recently announced that it will move and reopen at 749 Moreland Avenue, C202, in Ormewood Square. Owners Steve and Margo Tockerman are moving the store into another second-floor space, so the Loft part of the name still applies.

Meanwhile, Decatur CD & Vinyl owner Warren Hudson runs a tight ship, with new vinyl releases stacked high amid rows of new and used CDs and box sets. And if he doesn't already have it in the store, he can get it with a quickness. Just ask.

There are plenty more shops in the northern reaches of the city: Comeback Vinyl is a small but well-curated record haven that's teeming with vigorous young energy on Main Street in Alpharetta. There are plenty of new and used rock, hip-hop, punk and folk records lining the bins. The benefits of a suburban location are that tons of folks who bought plenty of music during their pre-professional, pre-family years tend to let go of entire collections or rare and collectible records they've been sitting on for years before moving to the subdivision. It's good to check back often, just to see what's come through the door. Same goes for Mojo Vinyl Records in Roswell, which offers an impressive stock of signed records.

Sweet Melissa Records on the Marietta Park Square is the spot for those high-priced, hi-fi jazz records that you need.

Ella Guru Record Shop sits on the cusp of Decatur's Leafmore, Oak Grove and Sagamore Hills neighborhoods and is one of the city's essential destinations for classic or obscure rock nuggets, country gold, hip-hop 12 inches and serious jazz and indie rock scores.

There are too many other shops to get into much more detail here, but I would be remiss if I didn't highlight one of the city's latest and greatest new record stores, Disorder Vinyl. The shop's owner, Yoonsang Doo, brings an expertly curated selection of hardcore, jazz, hip-hop, punk and alternative rock titles to the rising Summerhill neighborhood. Disorder's arrival amid the city's waning pandemic days speaks to the demand for more record stores while all brick-and-mortar retail outlets struggle for survival.

After all, it was the record stores that drew us out of our homes as soon as the city's quarantine orders started lifting. More on that later.

These tales from Atlanta's record store underground present an oral history of the city's rock music scene, as witnessed through the lens of Criminal Records, Fantasyland, Wax'n'Facts and many more. This is a rock-centric take on a town that's often praised and admired around the world as a hip-hop mecca. Here, the secret history of the underdogs—outsiders living among outsiders—are told. From Jarboe of SWANS to William DuVall of Alice in Chains and Neon Christ, to Kelly Hogan and those surly guys behind the counter at Wuxtry, all were drawn by the irresistible lure of vinyl records. Like so many, each developed a deeper relationship with their communities and honed their identities in these cluttered spaces, leaving an indelible mark on the culture of Atlanta. Here, in their own voices, their stories are told.

AS A TEENAGER GROWING up in Iowa, just across the river from Omaha, Nebraska, I remember when Pearl Jam released its debut album in the summer of 1991. The media was obsessed with the fact that the group pressed an LP along with the CDs and cassettes. At seemingly every turn, I saw stories in the *Omaha World Herald*, *Alternative Press* and even the *New York Times*, about how vinyl was "making a comeback."

At the time, I had already made the plunge into the worlds of punk, post-punk, industrial music, indie rock, countrypolitan, folk music and so on. A lot of the music that I wanted to hear existed only on used LPs that I'd routinely dig for at the record shops around Omaha. And it was usually cheap! Drastic Plastic and the Antiquarium in the Old Market and Kanesville Kollectibles in Council Bluffs were my haunts. There were long stretches when I went to at least one, if not all of them, every day if I could. If I had somehow earned a little extra money, I'd drop it on import pressings of albums, sometimes just because the cover art caught my attention.

That vinyl "comeback" has never really ceased, as far as I can tell. Every few years, it seems, I come across a new story about how physical media is once again on the rise.

RETURNING TO THE ALL-IMPORTANT question of why write a book about Atlanta record stores, the truth is that you get a singularly unique perspective on a city's history, its culture and its personality when viewed through the record store's front window. I have often said that if you want to understand a society or a culture, just take a look at its pop culture, and music has always remained right there on the frontlines.

Weimar cultural critic Siegfried Kracauer often referred to the notion of a "blizzard of images"—sensory overload—getting in the way of deeper connections with art and media in the contemporary world. There's too much choice, too much information bogging down the process of making a meaningful connection. I often invoke this when talking about the chaotic glut of music being thrown at the world in an age when everyone has Spotify, Bandcamp, Tidal, Apple Music, you name it, right in the palms of their hands.

The entry points for engaging with an artist or a narrative are easier to access than ever before. But every so often, a deeper connection is lost in the noise. Attention spans are growing shorter with each new update to our phone's operating system. As a result, artists struggle or they rely on pure bombast to capture someone's ears in the ten-second clips flashing by our faces, which are all ultimately lost in the mindless scroll of Instagram and Facebook stories. But vinyl records are forever.

IT IS IN A city's nature to change. Neighborhoods flip; gentrification shuffles communities around like pieces on a game board. Cultures rise and disappear as the urban landscape is ripped apart and reshaped.

In Atlanta, the well-oiled machines of change move at a disarmingly rapid pace. And while the scenery changes, record stores remain. Wuxtry, Wax'n'Facts and Fantasyland—even though Fantasyland has moved around to a few different locations over the years—look pretty much the same as they did in the 1990s, in the '80s or even the late '70s.

Each of these shops is a time capsule, and each one has developed its own repertoire of regular characters and an over-the-counter banter that would send playwright and filmmaker David Mamet running for the door screaming (or taking notes for a *Glengarry Glen Ross* sequel). It's all in the spirit of surly fun and camaraderie, though.

It's a battle-proven, old-world atmosphere that suits a timeless medium for music that has survived changing trends, changing cityscapes and other formats muscling their way into the scene.

Cassette tapes, 8-tracks, CDs, downloads and streaming services have all tried to render vinyl records obsolete. But records just won't go away, and people remain tethered to their favorite records stores. What brings them all together is the music, the physical media and the ritual of getting their hands dirty while scouring through the bins, looking for a diamond in the rough. Taking their finds home, cleaning them up and gently setting the needle down into those deep black grooves is something akin to a meditative practice.

Maybe you went into the store looking for something specific. Maybe not. Regardless, an album cover, a title, an artist's name or a song will strike at the synapses like a copperhead that you didn't see hiding in the ivy—in a good way!

People have different tastes, and no two people listen to music the same way, even when they're rubbing elbows with strangers in the same small piece of commercial retail space, sometimes for decades. Sometimes they remain strangers—competition looking for the same records. But oftentimes their stories overlap.

It's in these record stores where a truly secret history of Atlanta lies and where a parade of seemingly disparate artists such as one-time local musical acts ranging from RuPaul, OutKast, Neon Christ, the Brains, the Hampton Grease Band, Black Lips, Marion Brown, the Indigo Girls, Algiers, Cat Power, William Bell, Drivin N Cryin, Abner Jay, the Coathangers, Mastodon, Kelly Hogan, the Black Crowes, Deerhunter, Blackberry Smoke, Jerry Reed, Goodie Mob, Zac Brown, Lil Nas X, Butch Walker, Blind Willie McTell and so many others find common ground with one another while tapping into the much larger universe of music.

IT'S THE LATTER NAME on the list—Piedmont blues legend Blind Willie McTell—who, late one night in the fall of 1956, with his twelve-string guitar in hand, shuffled into Ed Rhodes's record shop on the corner of Thirteenth and Peachtree Streets, where a recording machine was set up. There, McTell captured what would become his *Last Session* LP. And indeed, it was the final recording he made before dying just a few years later.

That night in the record shop, McTell eased his way into a ragtime love song, "Baby, It Must Be Love." Then came "The Dyin' Crapshooters Blues," a cautionary murder ballad filled with macabre wit and wisdom that he penned about a friend with a gambling problem who died in his arms after being shot by police.

He sang "Kill It, Kid," "Early Life," "A Married Man's a Fool," "Wabash Cannonball," "Pal of Mine" and more; each of his words and every pluck of his nickel-plated steel strings are delivered with a frail intimacy that exceeds his typically soft and expressive singing and strumming.

McTell was an old man, fast approaching the end of his life. He loved corn whiskey, and he downed a jar while offering brief but bewitching tales behind a few of his songs.

He was something of a Ponce de Leon Avenue fixture at the time. He would go out at night to make money to buy more whiskey by singing and playing his guitar for young lovers parked in cars in the shadowy lot behind the Blue Lantern Club, where the Local bar now stands. Soon, even the Local will disappear with much of the rest of Ponce's old familiar places—

The *Last Session* LP by Blind Willie McTell, released in 1960. *Prestige Bluesville.*

all casualties to a never-ending wave of condos and soulless, live-work-play monstrosities being erected throughout the city.

Between each song that was captured for *Last Session*, McTell engages with an invisible audience, maybe just an occasional shopper milling about the store. Maybe he's talking with no one at all. Between each haunting number, paired with the album's liner notes, *Last Session* paints a picture of a postwar Atlanta cityscape that no longer exists in time or space. The physical place that once housed Rhodes's record shop bears no resemblance to the bustling scene where McTell performed on street corners. It is forgotten history, but it was documented by a record shop owner for record shoppers to stumble upon nearly seventy years later and be transported through layers of time, to that fleeting moment of the past while the record spins.

I found my well-worn copy of *Last Session* at Wax'n'Facts, filed under M. It was a happy, accidental discovery that underscores the magic and the power of an album's liner notes. This is an entire other dimension of the listening experience that's lost when streaming music through one's phone or computer.

Last Session, along with countless other records are filed alphabetically, binding everyone from six-fingered blues guitarist Hound Dog Taylor to pop diva Taylor Swift—all with titles that are just waiting to be unearthed and examined, like musical and cultural archaeology.

OF COURSE, ALL OF this ties right back to the tactile experience, which you'll read plenty about in the pages to come. But most importantly, it's the people you encounter at these record stores, both behind the counter and while digging through the crates, who define the culture and make record stores timeless institutions in this city.

Record stores have played indelible roles in many peoples' lives. While I was having conversations with people for this book, so many of them told stories about riding MARTA for hours when word spread that a new album that they wanted had come out. Others made secret stops when they were first given the keys to the family car and told to run one fast errand. Making their way to the record stores became part of establishing their early routines, or it's how they learned to navigate Atlanta's twisted side streets to avoid traffic along the way.

This book is by no means a scientific endeavor. Certain truly great and beloved shops like Red Beans and Rice and Dumpster Dive along with chain stores, like Tower and Record Bar, have been relegated to the margins here.

It's easy to get precious about this subject matter. But for this book, I let the conversations lead the way, allowing for a tight focus on the independent shops that the city has spawned.

This is a collection of people telling their stories as they remember them, revealing a diversity of experiences of Atlanta's musical culture that were made possible within these brick-and-mortar repositories.

1

IN THE BEGINNING

AN ORAL HISTORY OF WAX'N'FACTS AND ATLANTA'S ROCK 'N' ROLL UNDERGROUND

On April 7, 1971, Hampton Grease Band's one and only album, *Music to Eat*, was released on Columbia Records. Upon arrival, the album's tangled and colorful blend of lively avant-garde rock 'n' roll presented a bizarre anomaly for southern rock and for the rest of the world as well. The group was fronted by Colonel Bruce Hampton, flanked by drummer Jerry Fields, bass player Mike Holbrook and guitarists Harold Kelling and Glenn Phillips. Hampton Grease Band had earned a reputation as Georgia kin to Captain Beefheart and Frank Zappa, albeit a much stranger musical ensemble than the Grateful Dead or their Peach State peers the Allman Brothers Band. The ramshackle improvisation, lyrical antics—words pulled randomly from encyclopedia pages—and the twisted tales being told in songs such as "Maria," "Hey Old Lady and Bert's Song" and "Major Bones" stamp in time a milestone for the old, weird South. Over the years, Phillips continued carving out a singular and largely instrumental body of guitar-centric compositions, landing him early deals with Caroline and Virgin Records. His ecstatic whirlwind songs reveal an abstract narrative reconciling a lifetime of confusion, vulnerability and ultimately triumph.

For Phillips, this lifelong journey into music began taking shape when his older brother Charlie got hired to work in a strip mall record shop in the mid-1960s. It was a defining moment for Phillips and for many other people as well, breathing life into an ongoing underground rock scene that still holds a secret sway over Atlanta.

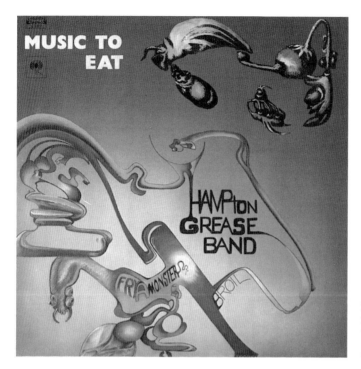

Music to Eat, the Hampton Grease Band's 1971 LP. *Columbia/Real Gone Music.*

The Hampton Grease Band, photo taken from the backside of *Music to Eat*. *Columbia/Real Gone Music.*

GLENN PHILLIPS: My brother Charlie Phillips, who was the original bass player in Hampton Grease Band, had, as far as I know, one of the first independent record stores in Atlanta. It was located near where the golf course comes to a point, where Lake Forest Drive and Powers Ferry come up and Powers Ferry connects with Roswell Road. It was just a strip mall, and the record shop was next to a drugstore and an ice cream shop.

Everyone from the Hampton Grease Band went to high school together at a place called William Franklin Dykes High in the Chastain Park area. It's now called Sutton Middle School.

Dykes held its graduation at Chastain Park Amphitheater every year. That's where the Hampton Grease Band had the very first band job that we ever played. It was a battle of the bands, hosted by WAGA-TV weatherman Guy Sharpe. That was the first time that I ever played live in my life! At Chastain Amphitheater!…No pressure! [laughs]

Charlie got a job working in this little record store in that strip mall. I think the actual name was Northside Records, but we all called it Charlie's Record Shop, because Charlie was the guy!

It was just one of those tiny little cubes in the strip mall—he loved music, and he loved that shop. It was there that he single-handedly exposed me and everybody in the Grease Band to tons and tons of music. He got the job working there in the mid '60s, and he was so successful that the owner said, "I'm opening up another store. You run this one, and you do whatever you want with it. Run it as you please."

The store was a world unto itself. Charlie had free rein to order any album that he wanted. He would spend hours combing through *Billboard Magazine* and every other music magazine that he could get his hands on and bring in any band that came out in the '60s. At the time, there was no underground rock scene in Atlanta. It wasn't like New York or the West Coast. The only place in the city where you could find anything like what you could find in those places was in this little store near Chastain Park.

Help Wanted: a North Side Record Shop ad that appeared in the *Atlanta Journal-Constitution* circa 1971.

Glenn Phillips in the early '70s. *Photo by Richard Perez.*

The shop became the center of the northeast Atlanta music scene. It is essentially where the Hampton Grease Band formed. All the guys from the band Radar would come over from Sandy Springs to hang out, and bands would play on the sidewalk in front of the shop. Bands would ask if they could come play, and Charlie would always say yes. It wasn't a regular thing, and it wasn't a band promoting a record. It was just a local neighborhood scene.

Every independent record that came out back then was at Charlie's shop a solid year before they were in any other record stores in Atlanta. That is where we all went to discover everything from jazz records like John Coltrane's *A Love Supreme* and Indian classical music, like Ravi Shankar *At the Monterey International Pop Festival,* to the rock records that we now think of as defining the era. Charlie had the *Velvet Underground & Nico* album in the store the day it came out. He had the Doors record the day it came out, long before they had a radio hit with "Light My Fire." He was bringing all of these records that we now consider to be iconic—Jimi Hendrix, Paul Butterfield—and getting them into people's hands.

When people went in there looking for a specific record, he would say, "Listen, you don't want *that* record. You want *this* record!" He would sell them this stuff and say, "Bring it back if you don't like it."

C is for Cookie! Wax'n'Facts co-owner Danny Beard, posing with a rare find in 2016. *Photo by Chad Radford.*

DANNY BEARD, CO-OWNER OF WAX'N'FACTS RECORDS: One of the records that I remember buying there [Northside Records] was *Projections* by the Blues Project. Al Cooper was in the Blues Project. It was a New York group, and *Projections* was the one. "Flute Thing" is on that record, and Danny Kalb was singing and playing guitar.

We lived maybe five or six blocks away from Chastain Park. My parents moved to a place off of Powers Ferry Road. My mom's idea was that they would send us to Dykes, which was a "good" public school. I don't know that it would've been that good, but it would've been fun. At any rate, we went to Westminster. I was the youngest of four.

Northside Records was at the end of Wieuca Road. They had a Morrison's or some kind of cafeteria thing there. My family used to go eat there every few weeks. When we were there, my brother and I would eat quickly so that we could run over to the record store, and we would end up buying stuff there because it was like $1.40 for a record. At Kmart it was $1.98. We're talking 1967 here.

My brother and I would pool our money, maybe borrow a quarter from our mother, and buy records. My brother was older than me, and when he went off to college, he took with him all of those records that I had partially bought, which was annoying.

Back then, I got to know Charlie from playing basketball. Years later, he became a lawyer. My ex-wife was a lawyer, and when our oldest son was born, she was trying to go back to work at the Mediation Center in Inman Park, near the Trolley Barn. Charlie ran it, and he hired her to do a few cases. That was probably in the early to mid-'90s. I didn't know until many years later that it was Charlie who ran that record shop.

GLENN PHILLIPS: Charlie went on to become a music lawyer and had a fairly successful career working with bands like Drivin N Cryin and the Georgia Satellites. He was with the Satellites when they had the big hit "Keep Your Hands to Yourself" and dealt with negotiating deals, marketing stuff and all that. He helped me when I signed my contract with Virgin Records. He stayed involved with music, and he played for a long time, but Charlie was more of a scene maker. He had a passion for music.

Charlie Phillips died in November 2011. He was sixty-five years old.

There certainly were other record stores in the city, like Jim Sallee's Record Shop in Buckhead. But Charlie's shop was like an *Alice in Wonderland* trip, going into a place where none of this stuff existed anywhere. Of course, within a couple of years, all this music exploded and became a national thing. It was a big deal when *Life* magazine had Jefferson Airplane on the cover in 1968. It was around that time that everything started filtering out to other record stores, and you could go to other places. But for a good eighteen months at least—maybe a couple of years—this is where we all went because this was the first place where you could find any of this music.

HARRY DEMILLE, CO-OWNER OF WAX'N'FACTS: One shop that I really liked going to was Melody Music downtown. It was underneath the historic Coca-

Cola sign, by Five Points and Woodruff Park. There was a Russell Stover candy shop that looked really neat in a kind of '50s deco way. Melody Music was next door or a few doors down on that piece of land.

They had a lot of things that you just didn't see at Clark's in Decatur or at Jim Sallee's. They would have the whole ESP-Disk' discography. You'd go in and say, "What's this band? The Fugs? Weird." I remember going in there and hearing someone ask if they could see the records by Doug Clark and the Hot Nuts, and the guy literally pulled one of each of their records out from behind the counter.

Peaches Records & Tapes opened in 1975, near the intersection of Peachtree Hills and Peachtree Road. The chain, which originally opened in Los Angeles around 1963, was the size of a grocery store and said to stock $500,000 in music at any given moment, which meant it was the place to find albums by any artist known to mankind. Countless touring artists that were passing through Atlanta would hold in-store signings and appearances there. Some artists visiting the store, including ZZ Top, the Allman Brothers, Willie Nelson and more, set their handprints in wet cement in the sidewalk outside the store.

The physical space no longer exists, but the store's trademark wooden record crates with the Peaches logo covering the ends have become highly collectible items among record shoppers of a certain age.

JARBOE OF THE LIVING JARBOE BAND, FORMERLY OF SWANS: One memory that stands out is seeing Robert Fripp performing his frippertronics live inside Peaches.

He had an amp and other things on the floor....He sat on a low chair or stool inside the big front window of the store. He signed one of his albums for me.

HARRY DeMILLE: Peaches came around a little after Melody and was fantastic. I used to go in there for a couple of hours at a time, and I had the time of my life just looking through everything there. Atlanta had never had anything like it.

DOUG DeLOACH, LONGTIME ATLANTA MUSIC WRITER AND FORMER PEACHES EMPLOYEE FROM 1974 TO 1975: It was easily the equivalent of what Tower Records became years later. It had every genre, with lots of albums in those genres. Cassettes. Imports. Jazz, funk, classical, experimental, noise and, of course, rock 'n' roll. It carried top 10 releases, but it went much deeper, and

Jarboe of the Living Jarboe Band and formerly of SWANS. *Photo by R. Collins.*

it carried everything that was on college radio. The buyers were young and hip, close-listening people.

At least when I worked at Peaches, unlike any other record store that I ever went in, it was as much a spot for socialization as anything. We all loved working Friday and Saturday night shifts. The place was open till midnight

Oz Records print media ad circa '76. *From an* Atlanta Journal Constitution *ad.*

or 1:00 a.m., and everyone that you knew, who was going out to clubs and concerts that night, would stop in and you could hang out. I don't remember any trouble or anything getting out of control. It was a warehouse that had a bunch of records in it, where you could hang out with your friends.

In 1976, Oz Records opened three Atlanta locations: Buckhead, Marietta and Stone Mountain. Oz was another early adopter of selling new and used records. As the name suggests, the store's owners, David Kaye of Southland Music Distributors and Steve Libman, conjured up an immersive Wizard of Oz *décor, complete with mechanical flying monkeys that whisked customers' picks to the cashier at the front of the store. Over time, the flying monkeys have become the stuff of legend. Even people who were around the music scene back then but never stepped foot into Oz Records all know about the flying monkeys.*

JARBOE: I was a display artist there, and I did a lot of artwork. It was a part-time job during my college days. The flying monkeys were life-sized realistic faux monkeys holding a basket, and they were on a track system. The employee up in the castle inside the store put a cassette, et cetera into the basket for the customer and pressed a button. Then the monkeys traveled in the air on the wire through the store to the cash register.

25

BRAD SYNA, VARIETY PLAYHOUSE AND FORMER OZ RECORDS EMPLOYEE FROM 1978 TO 1981: If you wanted a tape, you could pull it out and drop it on a conveyor belt, and it would go to the employee working in the tape castle who would put it in a basket and have the monkey fly it over to the register. It helped stop shoplifting.

JARBOE: There was also a stage, and the movie *The Wizard of Oz* was repeated throughout the day. There was also a yellow brick road in the store.

MARK METHE, CO-OWNER OF WUXTRY RECORDS: I went in there once just to see this spectacle that everybody was talking about, and I thought, what the fuck? This is like any other corporate record store but with flying monkeys. I was already a little jaded about what I thought corporate record stores were.

On weekends, at some stores, actors would occasionally perform hourly dance routines to "Ease on Down the Road," adapted from the Broadway musical version of The Wiz.

Later, Oz Records opened locations in Birmingham, Alabama, and Fort Walton Beach, Florida. The Atlanta stores closed down in 1981.

Wax'n'Facts' inception altered the landscape.

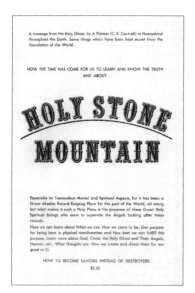

Is God in Stone Mountain? "Holy Stone Mountain" by C.E. Cantrell. *Courtesy Holy Stone Mountain.*

DANNY BEARD: There was also Mother's Music, down by Piedmont Park, near Peachtree and Thirteenth Street....And Jim Sallee's was around for a really long time. It was there in the '50s. We didn't hang out there too much because he charged "list price" for records. Instead of $1.40, like at Charlie's, they were $5.98, or something close to that. Jim Sallee's was right there where Roswell and Peachtree Roads split in Buckhead.

Harry and I were talking the other day, and I asked him about Jim Sallee's. He never really went over to Sandy Springs or Buckhead. That was way too far away for him. He lived near the North DeKalb Mall. He went to Druid Hills High School, and he went to Clark's Music in Decatur, which, he said, like Jim Sallee's, was full price. It was two stories. I went there once or twice. The owner was Harry Clark, and he or his wife knew my mother. I don't remember which, but they complained about all the publicity that Wax'n'Facts started getting.

There was also Cantrell's, which was mostly a bookstore, run by old man Cantrell—at least that's what we called him. He had a book on the counter that he had written, and probably self-published, called *Holy Stone Mountain*. He believed that God was in Stone Mountain. When Harry and I decided that we were gonna open Wax'n'Facts, I went to a lot of different spots around town. That was one of the places that had used records. But they just had them piled up on the floor.

Together, Danny Beard and Harry DeMille opened Wax'n'Facts at 432 Moreland Avenue on June 6, 1976. Since then, the shop has become a longstanding Little Five Points institution. It is the place to go if you want to be where the locals hang out. Since 1976, the shop's co-owners, Danny Beard and Harry DeMille, have kept the shop well stocked with new and used soul, funk, hip-hop, R&B, punk, country, folk, and rock 'n' roll LPs, used CDs, VHS tapes, DVDs, books and more.

DANNY BEARD: I went to the University of Georgia in Athens for my last two years of college. I had no preparation for running a business. I got a radio-television-film degree. I was mainly thinking about radio, because at Guilford, where I went for my first two years, I worked at the student radio station there, WQFS. Then I came down to Athens, and the radio station, WUOG, was just starting up. I did shows there: *The Big Band Hour*, from eight thirty to nine o'clock every Sunday night [laughs]. Get it?

So, when I got out of school, I worked at a small daytime radio station— WQAK, 1310 AM in Decatur. *Sophisticated music for the discriminating listener.* It was a big band station, and the owner was this guy named George Buck, who had a number of record labels: Jazzology, GHB, mostly New Orleans kind of stuff.

His son George Jr. is actually living in the house off of McAfee Road—near Candler Road—where they used to broadcast. Wadsworth Mill is the house, and they used to *do The At Home Show* with George and Eleanor from nine to eleven every morning. So I would go in at six and play big band music, and then their show came on. And I gotta say, it wasn't run smoothly [laughs].

He'd turn it on, and feedback would go crazy, and then he'd turn it off and go, "Oh shit!" And then they had these birds that were in cages that hung right by the microphone. They would just chirp like crazy the whole time! Louder than everything else.

It was interesting. So, I worked at the radio station for like two years, and I started at minimum wage, which was $2.10 an hour. This was the spring of '74. Then the station went gospel—Jimmy Swaggart. I wasn't into Swaggart, so I was looking for something to do.

I met Harry because he was friends with the band the Fans, who lived in a house on Seminole Avenue, right behind the store. My friend Mike Green, whom I'd known from Athens, became the keyboard player for them. Kevin Dunn and Alfredo Villar were the main two guys in the band. Harry and Kevin were best friends from Druid Hills High School. A spot opened up in the Fans' house, and I moved in.

HARRY DEMILLE: I rented the house on Seminole Avenue in January of '74, because I was tired of living in a really small place in Buckhead. We got a six-bedroom house for two hundred dollars a month. Later, the dining room became the Fans' practice space. The drums were always there. The mini-chord was there. My upright piano was there. There were usually some acoustic guitars lying around and some amps.

Harry DeMille, at home amid the vinyl. *Photo by Chad Radford.*

I wouldn't say we had a tremendous number of parties, and they were never set up in advance. It was always impromptu. Like one day, Russ King, the drummer in the Fans, asked Elvis Costello and the guys if they wanted to come over to the house and chat over a few beers. All but one of them came over. Elvis was banging on the drums. Steve Nieve was playing something other than the piano. They were all drunk, making noise and playing the wrong instruments.

When the Fans played at CBGB's, Hilly Kristal was such a huge fan that he paired them up with the Talking Heads. He said, "They're one of the bands that really fills this place up, and I wanted people to see the Fans."

David Byrne came to the Hotel Iroquois where we stayed and talked philosophy with Alfredo Villar, literally until the sun came up. I was like, "Sorry, guys, I *Kant* listen to anymore Kierkegaard. I have to go to sleep!"

One song that they loved to do at CBGB's was Kevin Dunn on guitar playing "Telstar," which was originally by the Tornadoes. Kevin played it really fast already, so you can imagine how it sounded when the record played at the wrong speed. It must've sounded like punk surf. I've always meant to play it at 45, just to see what it sounded like.

SEAN BOURNE, A GRAPHIC ARTIST AND LONGTIME WAX'N'FACTS EMPLOYEE: I'd hang out with the friends of the Fans. We were all going to art school at UGA.

The music scene was incredibly small back then. There were boogie bands, R&B bands and nothing like the Fans. They were a new wave band. They had all of those influences—Eno, Cale. In fact, Cale thought they were an excellent band. The Fans kind of brought us all together.

I'd take off on the road to work with the Fans doing backline. I was a roadie. They were one of the most interesting bands to listen to, but they were difficult for people to access. But they were the only band like them at the time in Atlanta.

When I first met the Fans officially, I had printed a T-shirt with an industrial fan. My style was to take letterpress and make random words out of existing words. Lawrence Ferlinghetti style. Sounds out of words. They loved it. They got me to do stuff with them, so I started working for them.

There were no punk bands at the time. The bands that were here were the Grease Band, Thermos Greenwood, Harold Kelling. They were the weirdos. The other stuff was like Banks & Shane. Everyone who was in the Brains and the Fans had steady gigs playing covers.

HARRY DeMILLE: Hampton Grease Band was just old-school weird. Radar was a straight-ahead rock 'n' roll band. They weren't ultraheavy like Hydra; they were more of a pop band. In retrospect, they had some really great harmonies. Two of them sang well. The Fans definitely had some songs that were lyrically too wordy and intelligent to be what I consider punk. Not that punk is not intelligent, but it's simple. There was a song, "Dog Street," where Alfredo just rants toward the end. That was a fairly punky stance. But they were more sophisticated.

Anything that was coming out of New York at the time was automatically called new wave. But if you look back at Talking Heads, Blondie, Television and other things coming from New York back then, did they have anything in common?

With the Fans, it definitely felt like there was something in the air, pardon me for that one [laughs]. We'd just gotten past all of the so-called Top 40 stuff, so things were moving away from bubblegum, Tommy Roe, real simple, sappy stuff. For a time in the '70s, if you wanted to hear something other than "Do You Want to Dance," it was pretty slim pickins.

DANNY BEARD: The space where we opened the store was vacant at the time, but it had been various things throughout the years: It had been a bar at one point, a bicycle repair shop. It was built in the '20s.

HARRY DeMILLE: The building had been a meat-and-three place for a while, although I don't know what years. If you look on the floor, you can see the bases where four old-timey diner stools were connected to the floor. And there were four big steel bolts that they sat over. I have one of them. I bought it from Mrs. Ed's junk store that used to be across the street, way back then.

The heating and AC unit is connected to the old grease hood line. When we first turned it on, the place smelled like one-hundred-year-old hamburger grease.

There is no other neighborhood in the city, at least that I'm aware of, that has changed like Little Five Points. It was the pits when we opened the store. It wasn't dangerous; it was just dead. There was nothing going down. Every fourth or fifth storefront was boarded up. Some of them had been for years. Our space had been. The owners were just overjoyed to have us come and be in it. I can't emphasize enough how run-down it was. The place had just been forgotten, right around the corner from Emory and Druid Hills and Georgia Tech. It somehow got last in suburban sprawl.

DANNY BEARD: Harry was working cleaning the Film Forum, which was a movie theater at Ansley Mall. It was owned by Bestoink Dooley, who was like Atlanta's version of Elvira. Bestoink Dooley was the stage name for George Ellis, and he would show old crummy movies. It's long gone now, but I think there is a Publix there now.

HARRY DeMILLE: I was the custodial engineer at the Film Forum Theater. I got to know George Ellis pretty well. As nice a guy as that mellow fellow who met you at the door when you came in to buy tickets. He was the host of channel 5's *Big Movie Shocker*, which came on after the news on Friday or Saturday nights, and that's where I saw a lot of the classic Universal movies, as well as a lot of the lesser-known movies in modern times. Everything from *Frankenstein* and *Dracula* to *Creature from the Black Lagoon*.

When he got tired of being Bestoink Dooley, he would come on as Bestoink's country cousin, Nurtnay Dooley. Of course, George was just having fun with a great southern accent. We were so young the first time he did it, that we had to ask, "Is that really George's country cousin?"

When we started Wax'n'Facts, we wanted to come up with words that were related to records and used books. There were never an awful lot of used books in the store. We kept them on bookshelves that came with the building.

Danny and I both looked at used records; we both brought in books. Fairly early on, it became obvious that people were far more interested in used records than they were in books. We bailed on books real early, like after maybe a year. Two years at most.

SEAN BOURNE: I started working at Wax'n'Facts around 1978. I had been working at an art supply store in Athens, and Harry and Danny hired me to help out on the retail side of the business.

At first, they hired me to print their bags. I was screen printing on the side, guerrilla-style shooting everything at the UGA art department, because I still had some hooks in there. When I decided there wasn't any money in Athens for me, they hired me. They knew music, but they didn't know retail.

I'd take off on the road to work with the Fans doing backline. I was a roadie. They were one of the most interesting bands to listen to, but they were difficult for people to access. But they were the only band like them at the time in Atlanta.

DANNY BEARD: We wanted to appeal to anybody who walked in the door. Because I had been on the radio station, I knew some people who knew that there was a record store coming, and this guy, Robert Jordan, was a great guy. He was a member of the Jazz Disciples—old Atlanta. They had a show for an hour once a month. Four or five of them rotated each month. These were all guys from Morehouse. Robert was in the store the first day we opened. We tilted toward the Black community.

It's still not the norm for Atlanta.…I'm not patting myself on the back and saying that we were taking brave steps, or anything like that. We were selling lots of Motown records and lots of jazz.

Over the years, a parade of regulars and occasional celebrities would come through the store.

Just a few years after opening the doors at Wax'n'Facts, Danny Beard launched DB Records, a self-owned and operated record label that remained in operation through 1997. From the beginning, the label tapped into a rich, new wave musical legacy that included releases by bands such as the B-52s, Pylon, the Swimming Pool Q's, Jack Heard (which included a young Thomas Dolby), Chris Stamey, Love Tractor and more.

DANNY BEARD: By 1978, the store had done okay, and we had more money than I usually would've had. I'd known Fred Schneider from the B-52s for a very long time. Since my first day in Athens, actually. He was running a record shop called Ort's Oldies. My first day in Athens, I didn't have my records with me. Like I said, my brother had taken all of our records off to college with him. So when I got to Athens, I went looking for records.

Ort's Oldies was up above what would have been the *second* 40 Watt Club. Fred was there, kind of running the store, but he was mostly playing Martha and the Vandellas really loudly and dancing around the room. Fred lived in Athens, but he had lived here, too. He's a record guy, totally. He still comes into the shop and buys records all the time.

The Fans had put out three 45s. I worked with them, carrying equipment. I did the sound, because there was nobody else to do it. Not that I was any good at it.…I went up to New York with them in about '77. Harry and I switched out going to New York with them.

One of the Fans' 7-inches spins at 33⅓ RPMs, and it was put in the jukebox at CBGBs. Most of the singles back then were pressed at 45 RPMs, but they wanted to get three songs on there—"Ekstasis," "Telstar" and "Lonely Girls." So when anyone played it in the jukebox it sounded like the Chipmunks. When I decided to put out records, I thought, *we're not gonna do that!* Let's do it at 45, not 33. I had seen what they had done wrong, but also

The B-52s debut single, "Rock Lobster" b/w "52 Girls." Released by DB Recs in 1978. *Courtesy DB Recs.*

I got to see what they had done right. I also saw that it was possible to put out your own records—because the store had done okay, I had the money to do it.

The first record I released was the B-52s' "Rock Lobster" and "52-Girls" 7-inch. We were friends and I said, "Let's do this!"

Bruce Baxter produced it. I was kind of the executive producer. I knew Bruce and got him involved. He mainly played in the group Thermos Greenwood who was Tommy Dean. He also did a solo record called *Middle of the Night*. Bruce was Thermos Greenwood's guitarist.

SEAN BOURNE: I printed stuff for the B-52s. Keith Bennett was doing their design work. I printed their shirts, and I printed the cover for their first single, but I didn't have the chops to make the fine print on the back. I did a couple hundred. I took one thousand of those sleeves to the printer, and he destroyed nine hundred of them. So there are only one hundred of them that I printed.

Pylon did a mass assembly job for their first album, *Gyrate*. Michael Lachowski did it. It was misattributed, and everyone got their feelings hurt. I did all of the stenciling. It should have said something like "art director," or "thanks to Sean for helping out."

Sean Bourne holds the first single he designed for DB Recs, Kevin Dunn's "Nadine" b/w "Oktyabrina" 7-inch (released in 1979). *Photo by Chad Radford.*

The same thing happened with Love Tractor.

I did Kevin Dunn, and I did the Brains' first single, "Money Changes Everything."

GLENN PHILLIPS: Danny put out the first Supreme Court record that Jeff Caulder and I did in 1992, titled *Goes Electric*, but I wasn't involved with Danny in a business sense. I was peripheral to that. It was sort of a different scene. Danny has told me that he used to come hear the Grease Band play, so he was aware of that stuff. But when the Athens scene came along, I had already become involved with Virgin Records overseas and was dealing with stuff over there.

Danny used to come out here to Brookhaven all the time. There was a big lot where they'd play softball games. Danny would always be at those, and he would always be at parties. So I knew Danny and was always friendly with him. I helped put the Swimming Pool Q's together. I was really close with Jeff in Florida. He was a music writer, and then we started writing songs together. Then he told me he wanted to put a band together, and I said, "I have a guy, the perfect guitar player!" I had given guitar lessons to Bob Elsey, who went on to be in the band. And I introduced him to Anne Boston, and they became involved with Danny.

I produced a demo tape that led to them getting the A&M deal after their first DB Recs release.

Over the years, Wax'n'Facts developed a reputation as one of the best independent record shops in town.

Kelly Hogan, vocalist who has worked with Mavis Staples, the Decemberists, the Rock*A*Teens, the Jody Grind, the Flat Five and more. She is a former Wax'n'Facts employee: I started working at Turtles store no. 34 in 1987 right next to Plaza Drugs. Then it enlarged and moved to the end of the strip.

Previously, I'd been working in aircraft sales for Hangar 1, a Beechcraft subsidiary, at Peachtree-DeKalb Airport in Chamblee. I got bass-ackwarded

Kelly Hogan (*left*) with Chris Stamey and Christina Eichelberger at Turtles Records & Tapes on Ponce de Leon Avenue circa 1987–88. *Courtesy of Kelly Hogan.*

35

into that job. I come from a family of pilots. My dad is a helicopter pilot. My brother was there learning how to fly a plane at a certain time. I needed a job. But I wanted to be in a band, and I wasn't meeting any musicians out there. I was meeting pilots and typing up bills of sales for giant King 300s—I'd type up $1,749,822.74, and I would always yell to the sales guys, can't we just round it up if it's over a million dollars?

That was my last real pantyhose job, where I had insurance. I couch surfed for a while, then I got a job at Turtles. And within a few months of quitting the airport and living in an apartment behind the Clermont Lounge, with no couch and no bed, I met Bill Taft and we started playing music together.

At first, we started off playing as An Evening with the Garbageman. He said, "I play with these guys on Monday night at the White Dot…. You should come play with us!" So I started playing with them. Later on, we started the Jody Grind. Bill also played in a band called the Chowder Shouters, and to this day, I have covered their song "Arkansaw Side" in my solo bands in the years since.

So I started wearing the green dress, working as a Turtles cashier. Then I started doing a lot of their displays, and I was pretty good at it. I won a couple of contests, where they would send us the record flats, and I'd get out the scissors and the stapler, and fan out Tracy Chapman's head a bunch of times. Then I ended up being an assistant manager. I have a curse. I can't just work somewhere. All of the sudden I am the assistant manager, and it sucks balls. Sometimes, I wish I could turn that part of me off and just be a minion.

My manager there was Tracy Blair. She and I would shop at Wax'n'Facts all the time. One day, they asked us if we wanted to work there part time, on the weekends. Of course we did!

So for a while, we were both working full-time-ish at Turtles during the weekdays and working at Wax'n'Facts on the weekends. Then Tracy's boss, the regional manager, told us that we had to choose, Turtles or Wax'n'Facts. They thought it was a conflict of interests, but it hadn't even occurred to us that we could be selling our promos or that there was some sort of nefarious deal at all. We just had rabies for music and working at record stores, and we liked the discount we got from working at Wax'n'Facts. That might have been '89 or '90.

I never took a paycheck home from Wax'n'Facts. Every week, my hold stack just ate up any money that I would make there.

But even though Tracy was the manager, and I was the assistant manager, both making money at Turtles, we chose to work at Wax'n'Facts.

Turtles was a Ticketmaster outlet and a video store. We always had to play the Top 10 releases, and we'd stack them that way. That's how I know the Basia album *Time and Tide* by heart. And we had to sell some Windham Hill records because they were doing well at the time. I *hated* playing the George Thorogood record, more than anything [laughs]. It was the worst!

Sometimes there were records that we liked: the Smithereens' *Green Thoughts*, Terence Trent D'Arby, Tracy Chapman.

Wax'n'Facts was diametrically opposed to that sort of thing. The store was way dirtier. Even though we swept every day, it's right there on Moreland Avenue. Your fingers would be covered in black grime at the end of the day. People would bring in records and say, "We found these in grandma's basement!" And they'd be covered in mold.

A lot of times we would say, "We can't sell these records!" Then two hours later, a person would bring in the same batch of records because they'd pulled them out of the dumpster behind the store. So when we refused records we would say please don't throw these away behind the store. Take them back home or somewhere else and throw them away.

When I started working at Wax'n'Facts, I was the friendly one. Sean would get so frustrated: There was one guy who would call the store every day looking for Latimore records. He would usually call at the busiest time of the day, looking for this one particular Latimore record. They would say, "Hogan, the phone's for you!" So I would always go and look. I kept thinking, gosh, I hope I'm here the day when we do have it, and then one day we did! He got down to the store right at closing time, and he was the sweetest blind old man.

Wax'n'Facts drew a veritable who's who of local and nationally touring artists. For a time, Fox Sports talk radio personality and former Black Crowes drummer Steve Gorman worked at the store. According to legend, it was there that his acquaintance Chris Robinson came into the store to ask Gorman if he'd join his then fledgling band, Mr. Crowe's Garden, which later morphed into the Black Crowes.

HARRY DEMILLE: I remember one time Randy Johnson, the famous baseball pitcher who was playing with the Houston Astros, came into the store. He was in town to play against the Atlanta Braves back when Houston was still in the National League. He was a down-home Texas redneck—a total joy. He came in because he was looking for a Led Zeppelin coffee table book that we had in paperback. He said, "I saw one at that Criminal Records place as a hardback, but they wanted $100 for it. My wife would get after me if

I spent $100 on a book." We had it, but he had a manager or handler type with him who was rushing him out the door. He said, "Randy, we have got to be at the baseball field right now! I'll bring you back tomorrow and you can stay as long as you'd like." And they did come back the next day.

Ironically, the book he wanted had sold to someone else that night. I said, "Ah, you should've asked me to hold it for you!" So I went to look upstairs to see if we had another copy of the book, but we didn't. When I came back downstairs, though, I saw two guys from Rancid walk in the door, and they shouted, "Randy fucking Johnson! Cool beans!"

They ran to their van to get a record to give him and to get something that he could sign for them.

After they left, I said, "Randy, I didn't peg you for a Rancid fan." He said, "These guys just gave me this record. Do you think I'll like it?"

I said, "Well, it isn't Led Zeppelin!"

KELLY HOGAN: Label reps would often bring people to the store. That's how I met Ice-T one day. I shook his hand, and he had the softest hands that I have ever felt. They were like pudding.

Björk came into the store—I think the Sugar Cubes were playing a show in town—and she was pushing a baby stroller. The stroller got stuck in the door, and I remember her saying, "Open ze door! Open ze door!"

One day, it was my day off, and I was at home. They called me; they knew that I loved John Doe from the band X, and they said, "Hogan, he's in the store right now, get down here!" So I raced to the store, in my pajamas. I put on a flannel shirt over my nightgown and drove up there from my house at 88 Waddell Street in Inman Park. And there is a picture floating around of me and John Doe, hanging out in front of Wax'n'Facts. He's like saying "Cheese!" And I'm there in my pajamas, and I think my eyes are closed. We have intersected a bunch of times since then.

HARRY DeMILLE: One of my favorite encounters was Burt Reynolds. He came into the store and was looking for soundtracks to some of Jackie Gleason's movies. They were friends doing *Smokey and the Bandit*. He had a driver with him, a small English fellow. He found the *Lucky Lady* soundtrack, a film he did with Liza Minelli. In his very proper English accent, he said, "Burt, I don't remember this one." And without missing a beat, in a very deadpan way, Burt said, "Neither does she."

Andre 3000 of OutKast (*left*) and Sean Bourne at Wax'n'Facts. *Courtesy of Wax'n'Facts.*

SEAN BOURNE: People always talk about record stores as in that fond memory of…. They come in looking for something they read about in *Melody Maker, NME* or something they heard on WRAS. When we started ordering imports, we were going through it like crazy. It was new music that people couldn't get anywhere else. They couldn't get it at Franklin's,…Peaches got into it a little, but we were doing it before everyone else.

We sold the *NME* and *Melody Maker.* Pre-internet you couldn't listen to things like you can now, unless you were tuning in to John Peel and BBC radio on the shortwave.

Wax'n'Facts was a social place, and everyone came in there. Chan Marshall from Cat Power used to work at the pizza place around the corner, so we saw her in the store all the time. RuPaul was backed by a couple of bands—Wee Wee Pole. Andre 3000 from OutKast still comes in from time to time. So do all kinds of hip-hop artists and producers. There have been a ton of hip-hop videos filmed here. Matthew Modine filmed a scene for a movie here.

I don't necessarily see it as the place where people would hang out and share ideas, but countless artists and bands have come in and got info from Danny, because he put out the B-52s and they were a hit. Danny knew something about record making. He was a big deal at the time with that.

In 2000, Darryl Harris opened Moods Music on Euclid Avenue in Little Five Points, just across the street from Criminal Records. Harris got his start in the music business, at first making mixtape compilations of the music he loved: mostly underground soul, funk, hip-hop, acid jazz and dance music. After working at Earwax Records on Peachtree Street, he created Moods to function as a record store with an intimate and welcoming atmosphere. Harris remains active in the local music scene, participating in events such as the annual Labor Day weekend House in the Park parties and hosting in-store DJ sets by the likes of the Dangerfeel Newbies, Monica Blaire and DJ Kemit. Kemit is the former Arrested Development DJ and manager, and creator of "4Evermore," the song made famous by singer and songwriter Anthony David feat. Algebra Blessett and Phonte. The song emerged as David's first top 20 hit R&B hit, which peaked at no. 2 on Billboard's Adult R&B Airplay chart.

DJ KEMIT: If people knew how much kosher hip-hop they could get at Moods, and soul, and classic throwback movies…I would live there if they'd let me. I get my *Wax Poetics* there. The owner, Daryl Harris, is a vinyl collector. For a time, he was selling a lot his own 12-inches of '80s boogie, soul and disco. The reissue CDs, hip-hop, Latin and Afrobeat and the atmosphere is what I like. They play music that makes you ask, "What is this?" That's what Moods Music is to me. A place for camaraderie and sometimes just a place to chill and hide out.

They also carry a lot of the new 7 inches and all of those Dilla comps.…The beautiful thing about vinyl is you have liner notes. You see who else plays on a record. Back in the day when you picked up a Coltrane record you saw Herbie Hancock, Tony Williams. You'd get into these other cats' individual projects and see how they move and how everything is connected. Herbie went from orchestral to swing and straight-ahead jazz. Then he went electric. People said Herbie's music was bullshit when he went electric, but it changed what we hear now. Daft Punk would not exist if there was no "Rockit." Everyone plays a role. Even critics can piss off an artist and make them do better.

GLENN PHILLIPS: We're talking about all of these guys—someone like my brother Charlie and Danny Beard, and all of these other people who run labels, worked in record stores and did all of this work. These are people who love music. They have a passion for music, not just to ingest it but to spread the word and to culturally affect their community in a positive way, and they are an essential part of this community.

> *In my darkest hour, Wax'n'Facts was everything to me.*
> *—William DuVall*

In the video for his 2019 single, "'Til the Light Guides Me Home," singer, guitar player and songwriter William DuVall walks along the streets of Little Five Points, the epicenter of Atlanta's underground music, arts and shopping, where DuVall's musical career began. Before he traveled the world playing both as a solo artist and while fronting Seattle's alternative metal and grunge outfit Alice in Chains, DuVall was on the bleeding edge of Atlanta's burgeoning punk and hardcore scene of the early '80s. First, there was his short-lived band Awareness Void of Chaos (A.V.O.C.). Then, in 1983, the almighty Neon Christ was born.

With the 1984 Parental Suppression *7-inch EP, Neon Christ became Atlanta's chief punk and hardcore export till disbanding in 1986. The era witnessed hardcore's high-speed and aggressive style establishing itself across the country.*

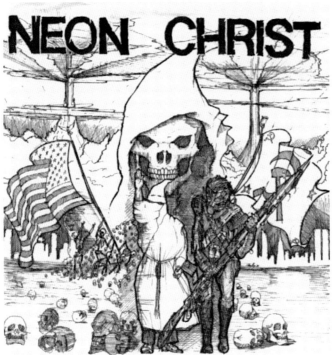

Above: William DuVall walking through Little Five Points in a scene from the "'Til the Light Guides Me Home" video in 2019. *Courtesy DVL Recordings.*

Left: Neon Christ's 1984 *Parental Suppression* 7-inch EP. *Courtesy Social Crisis Records.*

Neon Christ played dozens of shows, sharing stages with nationally touring acts such as the Circle Jerks, D.R.I., Corrosion of Conformity, the Dead Kennedys, Government Issue, Toxic Reasons, Minutemen and more classic punk, hardcore and thrash metal bands. The group traveled up and down the East Coast and played hometown venues including the 688 Club, White Dot, the Metroplex and more.

With DuVall on guitar and playing alongside vocalist Randy DuTeau, drummer Jimmy Demer and bass player Danny Lankford, Neon Christ consummated Atlanta's hardcore punk scene in the Reagan era alongside local cohorts DDT and Destructive School Children.

During later years, DuVall went on to play in various other hardcore, grunge, alternative rock and metal outfits: Bl'ast!, Final Offering, No Walls, Madfly, Comes With the Fall and Giraffe Tongue Orchestra. In 1995, he scored an honest-to-goodness radio hit when he co-wrote the song "I Know" for R&B pop singer Dionne Farris.

On the heels of releasing his second solo album, 11.12.21 Live-In-Studio Nashville, DuVall reflects on his early days in Atlanta and how a record store opened the door to the rest of his life.

WILLIAM DUVALL: I was already collecting records by the time I moved to Atlanta. It was my cousin Donald Copeland Sellers who got me into music and listening to records and collecting records. He moved in with my mother and me when I was eight years old and he was eighteen. He had a bit of trouble at home and needed a place to stay, so he came for what was supposed to be maybe a week or two, but it ended up being like two years.

When he arrived, he brought his small but very potent collection of records, many of which weren't very well kept because his home situation wasn't so fantastic. But the music was great. He had Roy Ayers, Santana, Pharoah Sanders, Weather Report....He had all kinds of stuff, and of course, the one that really captured my imagination was *Band of Gypsys*. That was the one that inspired me to start playing music.

Donald taught me about ecstatic listening. He was so inspired by and so enthusiastic about sound. We would put on a Hendrix record or a Stanley Clarke record or a Weather Report record, and he would say, "Did you hear that phrase?" He'd run the needle back, and he'd sing it to me, and he would point out something going on deep in the background: "Do you hear that little cowbell sound happening there?"

I learned how to listen to music through Donald, so I bombarded him with all sorts of questions about what I was hearing.

We never had a ton of spare cash, but whenever there was an opportunity, we would go out and hit some record shops, mostly underground shops and head shops that also sold records. It wasn't like we were always going into the established shops like Waxy Maxy or something like that. There was a place called Bread and Roses that we went to, and I remember getting Funkadelic's *Cosmic Slop* there for like three dollars. This was in maybe 1976 or '77, and that record was only a few years old at the time.

Then I got the bug, and I started going to any record shop that I came across. Whether it was in a shopping mall or anywhere, I always went in, and I would always try to find something.

There was a small shopping mall called the Waterside Mall, and they had a little record shop. Record shops were obviously much more common at the time and not quite the boutique things that they are now. I'd go in and see the new album by KISS, *Rock and Roll Over*, and that kind of thing.

Whenever I had saved up my allowance, or whenever I was with my grandparents—that was when I really would score, 'cause they would help out with the money—I started collecting. I was getting into everything from the Isley Brothers to KISS, and a little bit later I was getting into Van Halen as well as Ornette Coleman and James Blood Ulmer—*Tales of Captain Black*.

I should mention, too, that the reason why my tastes were as diverse as they were when I was like ten or eleven years old was partly because of my cousin Donald. But I was broadening beyond that because I had asked for and received a subscription to a magazine called *Musician, Player, and Listener*.

It started in about probably '77, and I was an early subscriber. The first issue that I received had Sun Ra and Funkadelic on the cover—sharing the cover. The next couple of issues that I received, one had Frank Zappa on the cover and the other had Brian Eno on the cover. But it wasn't just the cover stories. They had all sorts of great features, and they had all sorts of great record reviews, and they were as diverse as you could get.

And the writing was so good! They had Lester Bangs writing for them, Chip Stern. There were a lot of writers who went on to much bigger things—book publishing and all sorts of greatness—and they are well-known names now. I cut my teeth reading those articles.

I remember Lester Bangs had an article on the similarities, relationships and the synergies between free jazz and punk rock. It was such a great piece of writing. I read that when it came out and I was like, "Whoa, okay, now I have to go out and get the Stooges' album! And I gotta find the MC5! And I gotta go and dig in on John Coltrane and Albert Ayler."

When I would do my trawling through the record shops, I had all these names to look for. Back then, you could find the Stooges' *Raw Power* in the cut-out bin! I got *Raw Power* at a record store called Harmony Hut in the Columbia Mall when I moved to Columbia, Maryland, from D.C. You'd go in there and leaf through the racks and see a Mahavishnu album or something like that. You could go back in like a month later, and it would still be there. Eventually, I would get the money together and buy the album. So I had quite a collection before I came to Atlanta.

When I got here, one of the first things I did was ask around, "Where are the record shops?"

By then, I had already gotten into the beginnings of hardcore punk. At the time, my whole thing was that I wanted to get some folks together to form a band. Right when I made the decision to start a band was when we had to pull up stakes and move. So, I didn't know anybody when I got to Atlanta, which was a total drag. I was like fourteen years old, and that's just a tough age to leave your friends and to leave behind everything else that you know.

When I got here, it was like starting over from nothing—zero. The first safe haven that I discovered was Wax'n'Facts Records. I don't remember how I first heard the name, but I was asking everyone about what was happening here. At some point during my exhaustive search and interrogation of people that name came up, I made my way to Little Five Points. I think I took the bus, and I found it.

It was this place that made me feel like there was hope! I didn't know anything about Atlanta, other than what I had seen in the civil rights footage from the '60s....And, of course, the child murders; we got here at the tail end of all of that. So it was just a bleak time, and my whole perception of Atlanta was bleak.

When I found Wax'n'Facts, I thought, "Okay, there's this whole other thing happening in this neighborhood, Little Five Points. There are cool people here who like all the same things that I like, and they know even more than I know."

The people behind the counter were always cool. It made me feel safe, like I can make something happen here. I can work with this place. If they've got people like this here, then there's probably a whole lot of other things that I still need to discover, and I might just be able to find them through this place and through this neighborhood. You could strike up conversations with people. You'd see what they were looking at as they trawled through the racks.

It was like opening the door to everything that has happened in my life ever since.

Later, it became a hangout for all the guys in Neon Christ. We congregated there. I remember one time when Danny Langford and I stood and waited outside the door for Wax'n'Facts to open so we could get Metallica's *Ride the Lightning* the day it came out.

Metallica is an institution now, but in 1984, they were an underground thing. They only had the one album out, *Kill 'Em All*, but Danny and I knew their music because of the whole tape trading thing. We had the first demo cassette, called *No Life 'Til Leather*, and we had *Metal Up Your Ass*, that was like a live bootleg cassette tape that had Dave Mustaine playing guitar on it.

I was really missing everything that I knew in Washington, D.C., and I was trying to figure out what I was gonna do here, and how I was gonna do it. Wax'n'Facts was also the first place that I knew of that sold the punk records that I wanted. You couldn't go out to any old record store and buy a Black Flag single, but they had it. They also had the jazz records that I wanted. And they had loads of used records as well.

I met the two guys in my neighborhood—Ricky Jackson and Roger Maynard—whom I went with to form my first band, A.V.O.C. But when I met Ricky and Roger and convinced them to come over to my house, it was so I could play for them the punk rock singles that I'd brought home from Wax'n'Facts.

I discovered Wax'n'Facts in '82, and within a couple of years it became a staple hangout for me. I used to skip school to go there. By '85, I was driving a car. I remember one time I got ill with some sort of cold or flu or something. I was at home, at my parents' house, and I got a phone call from Sean Bourne at Wax'n'Facts. He said, "We hit the mother lode! There's an estate sale that came in here, and I think you'll be very interested in some of the records that came in."

So I got in the little Chevy Chevette that I shared with my sister, despite my ill condition, and it was in the middle of a downpour—it was just pouring down sheets of rain—I made my way to Wax'n'Facts, and they had boxes from somebody who had a major jazz collection. They had passed on, and their survivors brought the records down to Wax'n'Facts.

I had a freaking field day!

I remember Sean looking over at me at one point. I was freaking delirious, feverish and just crazy, and I was really excited! I was pulling stuff out with a vengeance, piling up records. He said, "Are you going nuts?" And I was like, "Absolutely!" We just had this great laugh, and I still own every one of those records.

I felt like I'd found my tribe, and it was so nice because those years happened to coincide with coming of age and gaining your first little taste of independence. You're learning how to drive a car, you can get around on your own and then it becomes about where are the places that I choose to go? Wax'n'Facts was always at the top of my list.

I lived in south DeKalb, so I used to take I-20 to Little Five Points. That was my first regular route. I was learning how to drive, learning how to negotiate highway traffic versus city surface street traffic, and I pretty much learned it all by going to and from Little Five Points.

Whereas other kids might be out partying, getting into this or that kind of trouble or whatever, you could usually find me trawling through the racks at Wax'n'Facts.

I remember one time, when I was like seventeen years old, it was maybe Valentine's Day. I wanted to get my girlfriend at the time something really special. It may have been her birthday, or it may have been Christmas. It was really cold outside, and I specifically wanted to get her the Rites of Spring record. That was a big record for me and some of my friends, and so I wanted to get one for this girl who was part of our Neon Christ crew.

I got there, and the store was closed. I remember going around to the back, and I could see Danny Beard through the window that was at ground level. He let me come in even though the shop was closed. He was probably doing the receipts or something. He let me in, I got that record and I managed to get it to my gal that night. Little things like that were so important to me at the time, and I will never forget it.

Even if Danny didn't have that store, he would still be in the history books. He was running his label, dB Recs, putting out B-52s and Pylons records, all while providing a safe haven for misfits like me.

I hope that Sean and Harry and Danny all know how important they've been to so many people. They have to know on some level, but I'll never be able to thank them enough.

…And the same goes for Wuxtry, Fantasyland, Criminal Records. All of those stores have really played a role in helping keep a lot of people on track.

I can't overstate just how important Wax'n'Facts was for me; to have that beacon of hope and coolness and music.

In my darkest hour, Wax'n'Facts was everything to me.

It was just the format of choice for the kind of music that I was most interested in getting my hands on.
—*Jesse Smith*

Jesse Smith promo photo accompanying his 2021 LP, *Lose Everything* (Beach Impediment Records). *Photo by Riley McBride.*

Jesse Smith is one of Atlanta's consummate record store fixtures. He is the driving force behind a string of 7-inch singles and LPs bearing the name of his eponymous Gentleman Jesse and His Men—or just Gentleman Jesse with his 2021 LP, Lose Everything. *Over the years, Smith has emerged as one of the staple songwriters amid the city's flourishing punk, hardcore, power pop and post-punk scenes. A quick look through his discography is highlighted by his time spent playing bass and writing songs such as "Phone Booth" and collaborating with Greg King on songs such as "(Your Love Is) Inside Out" and "Journey to the End" with iconic punk outfit Carbonas. He was the singer and bass player with hardcore band Hyena, and played guitar and sang with late '90s and early aughts post-hardcore acts Some Soviet Station, Paper Lions, the Kossabone Red and more.*

In recent years, Smith has spent much of his time working as co-owner of Decatur's seafood restaurant and raw bar Kimball House. He's also co-owner of the Shiny Dimes Oyster Farm, near Oyster Bay, Florida.

In the midst of so many musical and culinary endeavors, however, Smith still finds time to indulge in his other passion: scouring through used record bins across the city as often as his schedule will allow.

JESSE SMITH: The first record store in Atlanta that I went to was Wax'n'Facts. This is actually kind of shitty, but I went there for the first time when I was maybe thirteen or fourteen years old—something like that. One of the guys I was with stole a cassette tape. We were dumb kids, and I didn't steal anything. But I remember him stealing a copy of Redd Kross's *Born Innocent* on cassette. Personally, I feel like I've made it up to them for any petty theft that happened over the years.

Shoplifting or stealing was never my bag at all, but when we left the store and were walking down the street, he was like, "Hey, man, I stuck this in my pocket."

Anyway, that was my first real record store experience, and we were just kind of ambling around. Later, I came into the whole world of buying music from a punk rock angle. So, for me, I was searching for music where the only format on which you could hear a lot of it was on vinyl. I didn't start collecting records necessarily because I was into vinyl. It was just the format of choice for the kind of music that I was most interested in getting my hands on.

As far as other early record store experiences go, there was a small bin of records at a punk rock shop called Crash and Burn, back when it was right there by the Roxy, which is now the Buckhead Theatre. We would go in there to get our Exploited T-shirts, studded belts and other assorted pieces of gear. While we were there, we would buy whatever 7 inches they were carrying. I remember buying the "Live The Chaos" single by the Lookout! Records band called Filth. It was the early '90s, so I was buying a lot of modern spikey stuff—Rancid-adjacent stuff. There was a band called the Rickets out of Washington; I got one of their singles there. I had read about all of these bands in *Maximum Rock 'n' Roll*, and they had mohawks. That was all a winning formula for me back then.

Another place that was really important for me was Stickfigure Distribution. Gavin Frederick would just set up a table at shows and sell records. I was probably fifteen years old the first time I bought a record from Gavin. You could buy a single for two dollars, and you could buy a full LP for like six dollars, so it became an affordability thing as well.

At some point when I was a teenager, I was trying to figure out what's good about CDs. They're portable, I guess. But I would rather just tape my records—I had a tape deck in my car. Buying a new LP would cost me like six to eight dollars, whereas a new CD was like thirteen dollars. So I was saving like five bucks by choosing to buy the vinyl release. I could just easily tape it and listen to it in my car, and all of that worked out just fine. So that's kind of what made me move away from other formats.

Back then, I was going to shows three or four nights a week, and I would inevitably come home with something that I bought from Gavin—it was two dollars! There was a lot of emo stuff. There was a lot of crust and grindcore stuff. It could have been anything within that DIY range. I liked all of those things equally, even though my musical output leaned toward the emo end of things.

The Postcard series was a big deal at the time, so I would buy anything that was on Tree Records. Hal Al Shedad was a pretty big deal back then, and they were a part of that series—they did a split with Rainer Maria. The Get Up Kids, Braid, Cerberus Shoal and stuff like that. I bought Inkwell 7 inches from Gavin.

I also bought crusty records from him—Havoc Records–type stuff—like Civil Disobedience. A lot of kids that I went to high school with were really into doom, and anything that Felix von Havoc was in, like Destroy, Code 13 and stuff like that, which was a little crustier than a lot of what I was into, but I did like some of that stuff, too. Assück were like the gods of that whole world. So, I was buying a cross-section of stuff like that, and every once in a while Gavin would get in something that was a little more indie-sounding.

By the later part of the '90s, he was stocking everything from New York hardcore records like Citizens Arrest to Thrill Jockey Records releases by bands like Tortoise and Trans Am.

By that point, though, I was getting back into punk rock, but Gavin would always get in whatever. His store was at the C-12 South warehouse in the complex that is now called the Met. And it was next door to the C-11 warehouse where they had shows. Every Saturday, he would open up the

Jesse Smith on stage at the Earl with Carbonas in 2018. *Photo by Chad Radford.*

shop from like 12:00 to 6:00 p.m., and he had his own little record market down there. Everyone went there.

Gavin always took people's releases, especially the local bands, and he would get them into people's hands. He didn't care what the music sounded like. He had the stuff that he liked and that he wanted to release on Stickfigure Records, but he definitely made sure to sling Black Lips records and whatever the new crop of kids making music were doing. He would always say, "Yeah, I'll take ten copies and see what I can do with them."

These days, I will go out of my way to make the rounds if I'm in the neighborhood. If I need to buy candles for work, I'll go to Ikea and then make my way over to Fantasyland or Wuxtry. Just hearing what somebody's playing in the store....I mean, one of my favorite records of all time is the first Wall of Voodoo record, *Dark Continent*. The reason I even know about it is because I went into Wuxtry in Decatur, and Richard was listening to it. I knew who it was immediately because Stan Ridgway's voice is unmistakable. Of course, I knew the song "Mexican Radio," but I realized I'd never really listened to Wall of Voodoo. I was like, "Hey dude, just pull it off of the turntable. It's coming home with me!"

Back to Wax'n'Facts, if you're thinking about the history of Little Five Points in general, that store has been there for like forty-five years! It was open before the punk explosion, which puts a certain spin on it. Then, you can think about Little Five Points being the artists' neighborhood, which makes it a hub for subculture and independent culture in Atlanta.

Then, when you think about how Wax'n'Facts, by way of the store's co-owner Danny Beard, is tied to DB Records, and the artwork that Sean Bourne created for the label, and bands like Pylon, the B-52s—even though they're Athens bands—Georgia's indie music was propelled forward by DB Records. There are plenty of Atlanta bands to mention in there as well, but when you put all of that into perspective, you see that Wax'n'Facts is essentially still the same business it has been through all of that.

I still pop in there all of the time. I use Little Five Points: Aurora is my coffee shop. The Little Five Points Pharmacy is my pharmacy. Wax'n'Facts is my record store. I'll hit Criminal and Wax'n'Facts both if I'm making a day of it. But if I'm short on time, or if I just need to get some coffee beans for the house, I'll pop into Wax'n'Facts and look at what's in the new arrivals bins.

One of the big things about Wax'n'Facts is that they were hard pressed to adapt to the pricing changes during whatever you want to call this vinyl boom. They're dealing with a lot of used records, and it seems like there are billions of them coming through the door every day. That stack behind the counter just never dwindles.

They're always working uphill to get that stack down. At the beginning of the pandemic, I was like, "Holy crap, it's the lowest I've ever seen it, this is incredible! They're finally getting caught up!" And then once things started getting back to normal in the sense that people felt okay about being out of their houses and could navigate the pandemic in a safe way, all of a sudden, the record piles were bigger than ever!

I don't think it will ever change. They're never gonna fix the hole in the ceiling over by the later alphabet soul section. They'll always have to move the R through Z soul records when it's raining, which is charming as hell.

They have increased their prices just a little bit, which oftentimes I encourage them to do. I have gone in there and reverse-haggled prices before: I went in there and found an original copy of the first Spacemen 3 record. Danny's in the middle of pricing it and says, "How about $20?"

I'm like, "How about $80? You can get a lot more for this!"

He says $40, and I say $60. And he says he won't go any higher. So, I give him $60 for what is essentially a $120 record.

There's a sign on the door that can't be missed. It reads: "Enter…but at your own risk."
—*Whodini, "The Haunted House of Rock"*

NPR Music's hip-hop staff writer Rodney Carmichael began his career writing about religion in Waco, Texas. Later, he established his voice as the music editor and culture writer for Atlanta's once-great alt-weekly Creative Loafing, *taking a front-row seat to report on Atlanta's continuing reign as a southern hip-hop powerhouse.*

Carmichael is also a creator and co-host of NPR Music's Louder Than a Riot *podcast, which takes a deep look at the intersections between hip-hop and criminal and social injustice.*

His journey into viewing the world through the lens of music began as an intrepid young man growing up in Decatur, Georgia, wandering cautiously into the rows of the record stores in his neighborhood.

RODNEY CARMICHAEL: When I was a kid, the first record store I remember going to faithfully was a Turtle's Records and Tapes chain store. There was a Turtle's location in a little strip mall on Candler Road, right across the street from South Dekalb Mall. That was the spot! That's where I got my first hip-hop records and my first anything. My mom took me there because I was literally too little to be out in the world by myself.

That Turtle's was my entry point into music, and it was *the spot* from an initiate's point of view. I'm sure there were other independent record stores on my side of town back then, but I just didn't know about them. I was literally in second grade when I got some of those first records.

My first vinyl: my mom took me to the store and said I could pick out two things. One of those records that I picked out was New Edition's first album. The other one was a 12-inch single by Whodini, called "The Haunted House of Rock," which is interesting when you think about Whodini being a rap group. This was before they had even put out their first album, which is funny because their first album turns forty in 2023, so that gives you a rough idea of how long ago this was.

Turtle's was huge for Atlanta and probably the rest of the Southeast. There were Turtle's stores all over the city. There wasn't anything really unique about that location by South DeKalb Mall per se. But it was in my community. It felt like my neighborhood, and Black music was what you were going to find there, even though it was a chain. It wasn't until a little later when I became aware of more ground-level independent record stores in the city.

I wasn't a huge record buyer as a kid. I listened to a lot of music, but it was more like listening to that one or two hours that they played hip-hop on V-103 back in the early '80s. Or trading tapes with friends. But I didn't really start buying a lot of music until my teenage years. Even then it was pretty sporadic. But I started going into record stores more. I had a friend who lived not too far from this spot on Candler Road back in the day called Third World Enterprises.

It was really popular, and they even had TV commercials that you would see on one of the UHF stations, like channel 36. I can still remember the jingle: "Third World En-ter-pr*ises!*" It was definitely Black owned, and they sold everything from incense to other things that you might imagine getting at a spot like that…Bob Marley and blacklight posters and stuff like that. Even as a kid, I wasn't sure what it was—I'm not saying it was drug paraphernalia, because I wouldn't have known one way or the other back then. But they sold tapes, too.

I remember a lot of our earliest favorite tapes came from there; my friend would head down there after school, and sometimes I would go down there with him. He would pick up early tapes by DJ Jazzy Jeff and the Fresh Prince and stuff like that. We weren't into buying local stuff yet.

Third World Enterprises was only about a block away from where King Edward J's record shop was in a strip mall a little further up the road. We knew him as just Edward J. Landrum in the beginning, and he had the first really big independent hip-hop record store right there on Candler Road.

There was a whole scene of DJs surrounding that shop; it's the same camp that Mr. Collipark came out of—Collipark was really young when he was a part of that camp—he was going by the name DJ Smurf back then. Lady DJ was part of it. Even one of Shy D's early DJs, DJ Man, came out of that scene.

DJ Smurf *had* to be one of the last, one of the youngest cats that was down with that DJ crew, which was really known for the local mixtapes that they would put out. These were mixtapes in the original sense of the word. There was a DJ creating mixes with all the popular current songs of the day. But in this case a lot of times they were very Atlanta-centric. So you would hear a lot of Miami bass and all that shit that was considered Atlanta music at the time. You

Rodney Carmichael, hip-hop staff writer, NPR Music. *Photo by Christian Cody.*

would hear *some* Shy D stuff. But then they developed a style that they would use to adapt to any kind of music.

It was bass heavy, and they had these slow jam tapes that they used to put out where everything would just be slowed down. It was almost like the way DJ Screw ended up doing it in Houston, but without the chopped part, just the slowing down part. Everything was slow. They would take a nationally popular R&B song and slow it down even further and put all this bass on it. This is a style that was coming out of Florida at the time, too. They would have all these dope tapes that you could buy.

Sometimes you wouldn't even know who the artist was. You would just hear it on the tape, and everything back then was detective work. These days we take for granted that we were doing that kind of work because now everything is so easy to just Google and whatnot. But back then, you would have to figure out from some older guys or somebody that was more in the know, who was on this tape. But that was the whole thing with hip-hop at that point. Everything you heard was new; you were hearing everything for the first time, whether it was something national, regional or local.

There was mystery to the music, especially if it was local. Nobody was writing about it. They probably weren't going to have videos or anything like that yet. So all of that stuff was really word of mouth, and that usually meant it depended on how many cool people were in close proximity to your circle. At that point, I was too young to even go into a place like Third World or into Edward J's and try to have conversations with the cats behind the counter. I was literally just a kid. It would have taken a certain kind of kid who would have been bold enough and magnetic enough to have those kinds of conversations. But I was a nerdy kid going to the Catholic school a couple of blocks away. I had my uniform on. It wasn't like I was cool enough to engage people in the kind of classic record store conversations that you hear about. I was just looking for the goods.

I went to St. Peter and Paul Catholic School. It's named something different now, but it was on Tilsen Road, right off of Candler Road. Tilson kind of split in between Third World Enterprises and Edward J's Record shop.

Edward J is a preacher now, which I always thought was interesting. Several years ago, when they made that Atlanta hip-hop documentary that was on MTV, and Maurice Garland was a talking head in it, along with a bunch of other people, they dug him up. Aside from people talking about Shy D on the rap side, Edward J started DJ culture in Atlanta.

When you think about Black southern preachers and how they tend to have this rhythmic tone and style of preaching, he had that classic rhythmic way of talking. Back then, he was bridging the generation of the old school Black DJs that you heard on the radio, that had that whole vibe and they would be rhyming when they talked, and hip-hop era DJs. So he had this whole style and sound, like he used to talk on these tapes over all these beats. Back then, everything had kind of a roller skate jam type of vibe. The beat would be playing, and it would just be a hook or a beat that would be looping over and over again. Then he would just come in talking rhythmically every few seconds. It was really on some old-school Bronx jam, hip-hop type stuff, but converted down to the South. You could buy those party tapes at the J store. It was real cool. He had this trill, high-pitched southern voice, and he was creating something real special.

I used to get my hair cut at a barbershop that was in the same little strip plaza.

Back then, I was so much on the east side—wherever you grew up, you pretty much hung out there. It's not that you didn't go to other parts of town, but if you didn't have family or people in West End or Southwest Atlanta, you just didn't make it over there. I knew about it; it just wasn't really my zone.

I learned about Big Oomp Records years later, probably when I was in my twenties, and was starting to cover a lot of this stuff myself. Edward J was operating in the early to mid-'80s, and that was early for Atlanta to have a little independent hip-hop record store. Oomp came along after that.

I found out about Wax'n'Facts Records when I was a teenager—hip-hop introduces you to all of these classics through sampling. You hear Eazy E saying something like, "Put in the old tape, Marvin Gaye's Greatest Hits"… and then you hear Marvin Gaye through Dr. Dre's production, and all of a sudden you're like, damn.…My stepdad had thousands of old vinyl records that he wouldn't let me or my stepbrother listen to or even touch. But I would sneak in and do it, and I was so meticulous with it, where I could put it back the same way he had it and he wouldn't know. So, I found out through my stepdad that Wax'n'Facts was the place to go, where you could find all of this old music. I was quickly becoming an old music head, even though I was still just a kid. I was falling in love with reading the credits and seeing what was being sampled, and I wanted to hear that music.

If I could talk my mom into letting me borrow the car so I could go to Walter's shoe store to get some new shoes for the school year, or something like that, I would tell her that I was just going there and coming right back. But I would make sure that I went through Little Five Points and would go into Wax'n'Facts just to see what I could see or to get some old, classic tapes. They had all the old stuff from the '50s, '60s and '70s. There was just nowhere else at that time where you could get something like Marvin Gaye's greatest hits or the Isley Brothers.

I used to ride around in my dad's truck on the weekends, and I would go to the club parking lots where all the other kids would be playing whatever the latest hip-hop was or the latest *southern* hip-hop in particular. But I was bumping the Isley Brothers' *Greatest Hits*—a tape that I bought at Wax'n'Facts.

If I bought a tape, it was something really special. Even though I was consuming all of this hip-hop, I was consuming it through other means. I watched a lot of videos; I watched the video shows nonstop. I listened to certain radio shows nonstop. I borrowed tapes from friends a lot. But for me to buy it, it had to be something special, like something Ice Cube put out. Something to add to my little collection. I loved going into record stores and looking at the album titles and staring at the albums' cover art, but I wouldn't always buy it.

Word of mouth was everything back then, especially at the independent shops.

My relationship with Earwax Records was a little different. The main thing about Earwax was that I was in my twenties, and my hip-hop consumption was a little different at that point. Earwax was where you went to get tickets for a Funk-Jazz Cafe.

That was a must-have ticket—Funk-Jazz Cafe was a carnival of Black culture—and I want to say they happened four times a year. The cool thing about Earwax was that once you went in there, you could tell that this record store had a culture about it. It was like all of your favorite independent record stores, but it felt like it was on another level of the independent record store vibe. You would go in there to find a lot of stuff that you couldn't find anywhere else. I had a couple of friends that were real Earwax heads.

There was one person that I knew who actually worked at a chain and used to steal records and tapes for people. He would take orders from friends too, like you could put a list in with him and he would hit them up and bring back the tape. But we all had a whole different level of respect for Earwax. It's funny to think about, he was working at this chain store and robbing them blind. But when it came time to go to Earwax and get some Funk-Jazz tickets, or even to make a purchase, he would actually buy stuff from them, which said a lot about the value of a place like Earwax.

You would go in there and talk to the owner, Jaz, or some of the people who were working there, and you could just tell that those motherfuckers

Bella Reece flipping through the vinyl at Wax'n'Facts. *Photo by Chad Radford.*

were cool. They were almost as cool as the artists that you were buying. Jaz just seemed like a cool motherfucker. You would walk in there and it would be busy and you wouldn't want to waste his time with any unnecessary conversation. I got the same feeling years later when I started shopping more and more at Criminal Records. The people working behind the counter, even if they were all coming from a different culture, they all just seemed cool. Like that cat Caesar [DJ Swivel] who's worked at Criminal for years. He's just cool, and he was of the culture that he represented. I don't want to waste his time with some basic conversation about some album bullshit.

When you have to listen to a record all the way through, the song that you would normally skip if you were listening on Spotify, you have to listen to it. So even if you don't really like or even know the song, you get to know its place on the album.
—Bella Reece

57

In 2015, Bella Reece was just seventeen years old when she started working at Wax'n'Facts. She was a high school kid with more than a passing interest in pop punk, metal and hip-hop music. Immersing herself in the store's vast repository of used LPs was an eye-opening experience. These days, Reece divides her days between a professional nursing career and traversing the store's labyrinth of record crates that are bursting at the seams with music—jazz, punk, country, soul, electronic and everything else under the sun. Every day, she trades banter with curious first-time record buyers and veteran collectors, all while getting her hands dirty filing records and shuffling around the towering stacks of new and used LPs that span decades and musical genres.

CHAD RADFORD: Were you already kind of a music head before you got a job working at Wax'n'Facts?

BELLA REECE: Yeah, I was. And I still listen to a lot of the same music that I was into when I started working here. Mostly pop punk, metal and newer hip-hop. Some people think it's cringy music, but I'm into it.

CHAD: People do like different things.

BELLA: When I started working here, I would spend all of the money I was making on buying tickets to go see all of these bands that I was into.

When I would go see shows by bands, like Modern Baseball or Real Friends, I had become familiar with their music by listening to it on Spotify. My introduction to vinyl came when I walked by the merch table and saw that you could get a 7 inch on a special color of vinyl that was only for sale at the shows. Most of the pop punk and metal bands that I went to see had special records like that.

CHAD: Did you think of these records as being somewhat ornamental?

BELLA: Yeah, that is kind of how it was at first. Usually, if you get a full record by a band that you like, you have to listen to it all the way through. I'd listen to their records and think, *I already have this music on Spotify.* So the record was kind of a trinket.

It's not like I didn't know about records, though. My aunt has a ton of them, I have an Audio-Technica, which is what Wax'n'Facts sells.

CHAD: How is listening to a vinyl record different from listening to the album on Spotify?

BELLA: When you have to listen to a record all the way through, the song that you would normally skip if you were listening on Spotify, you have to listen to it. So even if you don't really like or even know the song, you get to know its place on the album. It makes more sense, and you have a better understanding of the whole thing. That, rather than just listening to my

Bella Reece, lost in the stacks at Wax'n'Facts. *Photo by Chad Radford.*

three favorite songs that I listen to while I'm driving, gives you a deeper connection with the music.

CHAD: You use the words, "have to listen to," almost like it's a chore to listen to a whole album.

BELLA: Well, you are kind of being forced to listen to something you wouldn't normally listen to. These days, since some bands' music is all digital, you can skip through it. As a result, they don't make cohesive whole albums anymore, and things are jumbled up. So oftentimes, I'll think maybe I'll just get this song on the 7 inch, if I can find it. Maybe a long time ago, 45s were just an early version of Spotify [laughs].

CHAD: You are the youngest employee at a business that's been selling records for nearly fifty years. Do you find that the regulars who've been going there for decades have accepted you?

BELLA: Yes, for the most part. Record stores are an older scene, and sometimes people get really offended if you like something that they don't like or that they don't know—or if you don't like or know what they're into.

But what happens more often is that some middle-aged dad will come in to buy big band–era records and say, "You're too young to know about any of this!"

Obviously, I wasn't alive in the 1930s, when Bing Crosby was really hitting hard…and neither were you. So can we just not?

CHAD: Did working at Wax'n'Facts change your musical tastes?

BELLA: Before I worked there, I wrote off disco as an entire genre. I'm kind of into it now, though. I'll hear the O'Jays, and I hadn't ever realized that a certain song was by them, but I've seen it at the store.

Disco is really fun music to listen to, but it's the music that my mom listened to. I didn't really know too much of anything about a ton of older artists before I worked there. So most of the songs that I hear when I'm working at the store, I'm hearing them for the first time.

I also really got into Blondie's music. We did an in-store listening session for something a while back. I knew some of the songs, but then I really started listening, and Debbie Harry is great.

CHAD: What have you learned while working at Wax'n'Facts?

BELLA: People who like records are really nerdy, and they like what they like…passionately! From the outside, people can seem like they are really jaded and grumpy. Like if you didn't play Magic: The Gathering and you walked into a card shop it would be kind of weird. You'd have no idea what was going on.

Likewise, there's a community here. Everybody knows each other. They're dorky people, and I'm not saying that I'm not dorky! I always felt like people judged me for listening to pop punk and new rap music. But everybody likes what they like! Some people have just been at it for much longer than others.

CHAD: Have you noticed more people buying records as time goes on?

BELLA: It's always been pretty steady since I started working here. A lot of young people come in looking for newer records, but it's kind of the situation I was in. I came in looking for artists that I knew but then branched out because there's this huge section of used music in the store, and you see all of these album covers.

2

A BRIEF HISTORY OF
WUXTRY RECORDS

I n February 1976, Mark Methe and Dan Wall moved from Carbondale, Illinois, to Athens, Georgia, for the sole purpose of opening Wuxtry Records.
For Methe, it was the culmination of a lifetime spent surrounded by music that started when he was a child. Methe grew up in Oak Park, an affluent suburb that lies just along the western edge of the city of Chicago, sprawling out seven miles from the Downtown Loop.

In the 1920s, Oak Park was home to jazz drummer Dave Tough, who is best known for performing and recording with big band and swing sensations Benny Goodman, Tommy Dorsey, Woody Herman and more.

Oak Park's neighboring municipality to the northeast, called Austin, had given rise to the legendary Austin High School Gang, a crew of young white jazz musicians who included tenor saxophonist Bud Freeman, cornet player Jimmy McPartland, guitarist Eddie Condon and more—all of whom pioneered Chicago's hurried sound that brought a bombastic edge to Dixieland jazz in the Roaring Twenties.

Of course, Methe wasn't aware of anything that had to do with Oak Park's local jazz lore when he was growing up. "My dad had a couple of Benny Goodman records, but all of the cool records in the house came from my older sister," Methe said. "She's the one who brought home things like the Velvet Underground's records, and the first Bob Dylan record. When everyone else in the house was huddled around the TV watching *The Three Stooges*, I was in the other room listening to 'Pretty Peggy-O' and 'In My Time of Dyin'.'…That's not meant to be taken as anything against *The Three*

Above: Wuxtry Records in Decatur. *Photo by Chad Radford.*

Left: Wuxtry Records co-owner Mark Methe in 2019. *Photo by Chad Radford.*

Stooges," he added. "But I'd already seen *The Three Stooges.* This music was something new to me, and I wanted to listen to it."

In 1966, Methe landed his first high school job at a record store in Oak Park. At first, the shop was called NMC Discount. In 1972, when the NMC shop went out of business, the store's manager, Val Camilletti, took over the space and christened it Val's Halla—so named because of the shop's long, skinny design, like the hallway of the gods.

When Methe graduated in 1970, he had earned a scholarship that landed him at Illinois College in the small town of Jacksonville, Illinois, thirty-four miles west of the state capital in Springfield.

"There was a Capitol Records pressing plant there," Methe remembered.

Illinois College is a conservative Presbyterian school whose most famous alumni is William Jennings Bryan, a former Nebraska state representative. He was also Woodrow Wilson's secretary of state and is, perhaps, best known for waging war on the teaching of human evolution in state-funded schools during the Scopes Trial of 1925.

"I didn't fit in there very well at all," Methe said. "When I went there, I fell in with the theater crowd, because they were the hippest."

Even the president of the school invited them to put on a production of *Inherit the Wind,* Jerome Lawrence and Robert Edwin Lee's 1955 play about the Scopes Trial. Methe laughs when explaining that he had no acting abilities but was enlisted to play Hamlet in a production of *Rosencrantz and Guildenstern.*

"The biggest compliment I received afterward was that nobody said anything to me," Methe said. "I cringe when I remember it."

Methe did, however, land a short stint working as a college radio DJ at Illinois College. He laughs when talking about how he used to sell records out of his dorm room so he'd have enough money to buy cigarettes and food. But the school's mandatory chapel, strict curfew and rules upon rules were not for him.

When he was caught hanging out in his girlfriend's dorm room, an activity that was not allowed at Illinois College, Methe was asked not to come back to school the following semester.

It was during this short stint at Illinois College that he met Dan Wall, who was dating his girlfriend's sister.

After leaving Jacksonville, the two ended up in the area of Carbondale, Illinois, where they both worked at an antique shop called Wuxtry. It was run by "an old hippie" named Fred Bozek who sold used paperback books, art glass, political buttons from bygone eras and other knickknacks. Methe recalls that when he started working at the original Wuxtry, there was just one small box of used records shoved into an out-of-the-way corner. "The place was kind of a junk store," he said. "But when I started working there it turned into more of a used record store."

In time, Methe amassed a large stock of records. He and Wall hatched a plan to open their own record store and ventured deeper into the South for a change of scenery and a fresh start.

Wall had zeroed in on a retail space in Morgantown, West Virginia, where they planned to open their own shop. But Methe had reservations. "I said, 'Gosh, you know, I don't really know about Morgantown. Let's take a loop through the South and see what else we can find.'"

The two hit the road together, driving an old Dodge they'd bought for twenty dollars. The car burned oil, and both the hood and the trunk were held shut by a wire coat hanger.

Soon, it looked like they would set up shop in Knoxville, Tennessee. But Methe still wasn't satisfied. "I said, 'I don't know how I feel about this town, I don't know if I like it here.'"

They looked at their road map and noticed that U.S. Route 441 was a straight shot from Knoxville to Athens. Wall remembered that he had an acquaintance there. "He said, 'Oh, I know a guy in Athens. It's supposed to be a pretty cool town, let's go there and check it out!'

They made the four-hour drive through the Great Smoky Mountains and pulled into town. "It was February, and it was seventy degrees outside, so I said, 'Hell, let's move here!'" Methe laughed. "It's a lot different from what Chicago is like in February, and we instantly found a location to move in and open the store."

The first person they met in Athens was a newspaper salesman—a British guy—named Brian Cokayne, who was standing at the intersection of Broad and College Streets. He was selling copies of the *Athens Observer*. They struck up a conversation and found out he rented a space at a goat farm nearby for fifteen dollars a month. He also happened to be married to a woman named Kate Pierson. "This was pre-B-52s' fame, although the band started playing music that same year," Methe said. "I remember Brian said to us, 'I know this guy who might have a place for you.'"

Through him, Methe and Wall lined up a small storefront at 110 Foundry Street, near what is now the multimodal station adjacent to the Classic Center.

There was one small space next door to Tyrone's O.C. that operated as a restaurant, bar and movie theater.

Tyrone's O.C. was one of the most popular music venues in Athens at the time. In a previous life, it had been a jazz club called the Chameleon. The "O.C." was an homage to its former legacy: Old Chameleon. But in the late '70s and early '80s, the club hosted alternative rock and post-punk music. Tyrone's O.C. served as an early haunt for groups such as R.E.M., Pylon, the Side Effects, Love Tractor and the Method Actors until it burned down in 1982.

Methe and Wall agreed to pay sixty-five dollars a month in rent for the space, and they paid their landlord in comic books, which they dealt in at the time.

They drove all the way back up to Illinois, bought a car for $500—a Crown Vic station wagon that didn't burn oil—rented a U-Haul trailer and filled it with "three thousand records, along with a whole bunch of other crap, and we moved to Athens," Methe said. "That was it! We tried to come up with a better name. Something! Anything! But neither one of us could think of anything better than Wuxtry, so we just kept that name. Three months later," he added, "we moved the store up to 197 East Clayton Street, where it has remained ever since."

The name Wuxtry originates from a 1942 DC comic book titled *Boy Commandos* story called "Liberty Belle," by Joe Simon and Jack Kirby. In the comic, a legion of newspaper boys aid in America's fight to defeat Nazi Germany. They stand on street corners selling newspapers, shouting, "Extra! Extra! Read all about it!" But in their thick Brooklyn drawl, "Extra! Extra!" comes out "Wuxtry! Wuxtry!"

The original sign they used for the store was an upside-down top hat with the word *Wuxtry* in the hatband. "The image was lifted from an old *Man Ray* magazine from back in the Dada days," Methe said. "Around the edges of the hat were musical notes. That was a design idea we took from the agricultural product Jazz Feeds. Food for farm animals."

It's worth noting that when Methe and Wall moved Wuxtry from its original Foundry Street location to Clayton Street, the Foundry space was taken over and used as an art studio by the abstract expressionist and portrait painter Elaine de Kooning, who was married to abstract expressionist artist Willem de Kooning. "I've always been fascinated by that," Methe said.

The shop initially opened on a shoestring budget. But less than two years later, the business had grown so much that the next step was obvious: open a second location. In September 1978, Methe moved to Atlanta to open another Wuxtry store in the North Decatur Plaza, where

Left: Wuxtry Records' Decatur shop in the early '80s. *Courtesy of Mark Methe.*

Right: Wuxtry Records co-owner Mark Methe running the shop in the '80s. *Courtesy of Mark Methe.*

it still operates seven days a week. "We always wanted to get a place right down in the Emory Village, but we never could get a place over there," Methe said. "In the end, though, I think that's been fortunate for us. We found this place, which lies at the crossroads of Tucker, suburbia, the city and Emory University."

After forty-five years, Wuxtry is one of the oldest continuously operating record stores in the state of Georgia.

Methe and his right-hand clerk since 1991, Richard Kuykendall, run the counter every day, buying and selling new and used CDs, vinyl LPs, 78s, 45s and cassette tapes. A young woman named Zoe Webb has occasionall worked in the shop as well, exchanging stories about albums with customers and bringing a contemporary voice to the shop amid decades of album art, dusty grooves and posters. It's a small staff, scaled back from the team of fourteen employees who worked the store throughout the '90s, but a minimal staff keeps the store nimble.

"The formula we wanted: find a strip mall with a Baskin Robbins! That was the wisdom passed down to us by Fred, who had the original Wuxtry shop in Carbondale," Methe added.

Wall still runs Wuxtry in Athens, Methe remains at the shop in Atlanta and they co-own both stores. "He runs things his way over there, and I run things my way here," Methe said. "After all these years of running the store, we're still friends."

Richard Kuykendall behind the counter at Wuxtry Records circa 2019. *Photo by Chad Radford.*

Over the years, the Athens store has received the lion's share of the media's attention. Brian Burton (aka Danger Mouse), Kate Pierson (B-52s) and John Fernandes (Olivia Tremor Control, Circulatory System) have all worked at the Clayton Street shop. Wuxtry's Athens store is also an essential stop on the Athens musical history tour as the place where guitarist Peter Buck met singer Michael Stipe and R.E.M. was born. But it was the Atlanta store where Buck first started working at Wuxtry while attending Emory University. Later, he transferred to the Athens store.

Richard Kuykendall started working at Atlanta's Wuxtry in August 1991, the same month that Nirvana's *Nevermind* landed on record store shelves. "It was also right around the time that Miles Davis died," Kuykendall said. "I remember so many people coming in and asking about them both, looking for records by both of them when I was just getting started here."

When the words *time capsule* are thrown around in conversations about record stores or anything else music related, they're generally followed by a starry-eyed pleasure cruise down memory lane.

Nostalgia is a double-edged sword; it's an endearingly human quality to gravitate toward fond memories of happier times, which are so often connected with music. But nothing productive ever comes from being a slave to sentimentality.

After all, punk rock, classic hip-hop, jazz, blues, soul, alternative rock and most other forms of music filling the crates at Wuxtry Records all put the tense in the present tense, placing a real-time emphasis on lyrics, allegories, melodies, moods and metaphors that can say something about the here and now, even if the music was written decades if not centuries ago.

When Jimmy Demer calls Wuxtry a time capsule, the inference goes much deeper than pining over a bygone era. Demer is an English teacher at Chamblee High School, but he first left an impression on the city between 1983 and 1986 while playing drums with Atlanta classic hardcore punk outfit Neon Christ. He also worked behind the counter at Atlanta's Wuxtry Records shop from 1990 through 1995.

In 2016, Demer produced a ten-minute documentary, *A Film About Wuxtry*, which is available on YouTube.

Working at the store left an impression on Demer. A quarter of a century after moving on in life, he still visits the store regularly to flip through the long rows of crates filled with used LPs. One afternoon while thumbing through a crate of '80s punk and new wave compilation LPs, he looked up to survey the room and said, "Wuxtry still looks pretty much exactly the same as it did the first time I walked through the door here in the early 1980s. Over the years, all of the other businesses in this strip mall have turned over—businesses have come and gone and made room for new businesses to move in and modernize their retail spaces. But Wuxtry remains as it always has." He added, "That is a rare thing for Atlanta. This store really does pack a wealth of history and knowledge."

Later, while mulling over Demer's comments, Mark Methe shrugged his shoulders and exhaled a long sigh. "Yeah, I guess that is kinda true, we haven't really changed all that much over the years."

Then he laughed. "Gosh, you know, depending on whose point of view that's coming from, that could sound kinda pathetic!"

Methe's tone falls somewhere in a gray area between self-effacing and brash old-school banter. He's a master of joking around and verbally sparring to a degree that might come off as intimidating at first, but only to those who aren't familiar with his sense of humor.

In 2014, I put together a Record Store Day cover package for Atlanta's former arts and entertainment weekly newspaper *Creative Loafing*. My intern, a young sophomore studying journalism at Georgia State University, called

A day in the crates at Wuxtry Records. *Photo by Chad Radford.*

all the record stores to find out who was having live bands, cold beers, DJs, special giveaways, celebrity appearances and so on.

She submitted her roundup of events and for the Wuxtry blurb wrote, "The store's owner Mark Methe says he *heard* that R.E.M. was going to play in the back of a pickup truck in front of the store."

Thankfully, I caught it before sending it off to the printer. When I brought it up the next time I was in the store, Mark laughed and said, "Well that's what I heard!"

"Mark is a funny guy, and he's a good character," Demer said. "I knew if I could get him talking on film, it would be worth capturing, and I could document who he is."

"Being at Wuxtry in the '90s," Demer continued, "I had never worked anywhere where your basic interaction was making fun of each other, or constantly criticizing, and making jokes. It took me a while to get that humor, and I would go home and keep talking like I was at Wuxtry—make my girlfriend angry. It really affected me, and it was a lot of fun.

"Then when I started working as a schoolteacher, I realized that it had become such a part of my interactions, but I couldn't do that with the kids,

Zoe Webb reaches for a classic album at Wuxtry Records circa 2018. *Photo by Chad Radford.*

be sarcastic like that. I loved working at Wuxtry and being a part of that. But outside of that environment, people aren't used to that level of back-and-forth on such a high volume."

In the store, fading newspaper clippings—obituaries for musicians and music industry professionals from throughout the decades—are taped around the inner doorway. Layers on layers of yellowed articles are taped one atop another, memorializing everyone from Colonel Bruce Hampton of the Hampton Grease Band and minimalist composer Tony Conrad to rapper Ras G. Appropriately, even Val Camilletti of Val's Halla in Oak Park has an article taped on the wall.

Richard Kuykendall, while perusing the various obits taped to the wall, sings the opening lines from Richard and Linda Thompson's song "Wall of Death" from 1982's *Shoot Out the Lights* LP: "Let me ride on the Wall of Death one more time."

Most people don't notice the obituaries until they're standing at the register or walking out the door. Inside the store, every inch of wall space, every CD rack, record crate and every other surface—even the ceiling tiles—are

The Wall of Death at Wuxtry Records. *Photo by Chad Radford.*

lined with band stickers, promotional photos, album covers and more bits of musical ephemera broadcasting a visual history of popular music.

The hellish flames and charred-black skeletons from Samhain's 1986 horror-punk classic *November Coming Fire* vie for attention alongside posters of Bob Dylan and Sonny Rollins. In the opposite corner, a cardboard cutout of Blondie's Debbie Harry wearing a pink dress circa 1978's *Plastic Letters* conceals cutouts of Guy-Manuel de Homem-Christo and Thomas Bangalter of Parisian dance music duo Daft Punk peeking over her shoulder.

Posters of Norah Jones, Nirvana, Dead Voices On Air, the Cramps and countless other band logos and musicians' likenesses are splattered throughout the shop's walls and ceiling like a Jackson Pollock painting—a multitextured universe of stickers from throughout the decades blending in with an ever-changing wall of new and reissued punk, power pop, classic rock, jazz, soul and alternative rock LP and CDs. DVDs and cassette tapes fill the glass case near the back. The store's inner motif is a swirling vortex of visual stimulation and a repository filled with entire legacies of every musical genre imaginable.

Stevie Wonder looks over the funk, soul, jazz and R&B records at Wuxtry. *Photo by Chad Radford.*

"It's something that needs to be documented because Mark and Wuxtry won't be around forever," Demer said. "Stores like Wuxtry and Wax'n'Facts in Little Five Points were *our* stores when we were kids. We would occasionally go into places like Peaches or Turtles," he added, "but a shop like Wuxtry is a cultural institution."

At the beginning of his film, Demer asks Methe: "What is the place of a record store in American culture?"

Methe shakes head and with a hearty laugh says, "I have no answer for that."

Fair enough. Maybe there isn't one easy answer when it comes to qualifying the record store's place in the modern American landscape. Everybody has a phone in their pocket, and the vast majority of music's recorded history is two clicks away. Easy access to such an abundance of music may have changed the masses' relationship with music.

But since the Atlanta shop opened in 1978, Wuxtry Records has survived by beating back the many challenges—Amazon, the iPod, downloading, streaming—that have doomed countless record stores across the country. Methe and Co. have stayed the course, survived, even

Richard Kuykendall shows off an 86 band T-shirt at Wuxtry Records in 2019. *Photo by Chad Radford.*

thrived on the merits of developing a real bond with the people who walk through the door.

There will always be people who look beyond contemporary technology and marketing exercises to engage with music on a deeper level.

There will always be those who want to get their hands dirty—musical archaeologists digging through crates on a search for a tactile relationship with music that came before them. Chance discoveries!

It is a truly adventurous spirit, however, who seeks to learn from someone else's taste and experiences, regardless of whatever barbs may come their way in the process. The reward: walking away with an armload of records. That's what makes Wuxtry a cultural institution.

3

A DAY IN THE LIFE AT
FANTASYLAND RECORDS

S ince the mid-'70s, Fantasyland Records has remained a constant pillar
of Atlanta's record store scene. The shop boasts tens of thousands
of new and used vinyl 7 inches, LPs, CDs, DVDs, baseball cards and
more collectible and hard-to-find ephemera, all tucked inside a labyrinthian
retail space. It's a must-stop spot for the classic rock, classic alternative, post-
punk, '80s new wave, classical, jazz and R&B titles lining the walls under a
multicolored array of posters.

Between customers checking out at the cash register, the shop's owner,
Andy Folio, and longtime manager, Mark Gunter, took a few minutes for a
conversation about a day in the life at Fantasyland.

CHAD RADFORD: Mark, how long have you worked at Fantasyland Records?

MARK GUNTER: I have worked here full time since 1982, but I started
part time in 1979. I don't remember if I asked Andy for a job or if he
asked me. I think he needed some part-time help on a Saturday. I think
that sounds right.

CHAD: Andy Folio, you've had the shop open since 1976?

ANDY FOLIO: Yes, that's correct. We opened the store in November of '76.

CHAD: I started buying records at Fantasyland when it was over on
Peachtree Road, right by the old LaFont Theater.

ANDY: At first, we had a tiny little spot over there next to where the Fellini's
was. Then we moved over into the middle space. At least that shop was a
little bigger. Then we moved to the end space, which was the biggest one

Fantasyland Records circa 2022. *Photo by James Joyce.*

Mark Gunter (*left*) and Andy Folio at Fantasyland Records in 2019. *Photo by Chad Radford.*

there. So we went from small to medium to large. And now we're extra large here in this current space [laughs].

CHAD: That kind of growth is kind of the opposite of what I'm used to hearing these days. The perception in the media, and on social media, is that running a record store in the modern era is rough because technology undercuts owning physical media. Music can be free online. You're competing with Spotify and Apple Music, along with Amazon, Discogs and eBay. Lots of people find music and records on their phones and on their computers now. I still prefer getting my hands dirty and digging through crates of records and CDs.

MARK: Yeah, and it's safe to say that pretty much all of the people who come here feel the same way, too. There is space for all of the different formats and technologies.

ANDY: But vinyl is the backbone of our business. CDs...not too much these days. But we still do sell a lot of them. We're about the only place in this part of town that still has any CDs for sale at all—new and used. There's Barnes & Noble, who has a small section of records and CDs, but we're the only independent shop.

MARK: And I think most people in Barnes & Noble are looking for books and gifts and things like that. When they see the records they think, "Oh, who knew they even still made these things?" [laughs]

CHAD: Where did you grow up?

Opposite: Mark Gunter (*center*) at Fantasyland Records circa 1986. *Courtesy of Mark Gunter.*

Above: Fantasyland's Peachtree Road façade circa 2007. *Courtesy of Mark Gunter.*

ANDY: I moved to Atlanta in 1971, from Greenville, South Carolina. I was twenty-five years old when I moved down here. I had no record store experience whatsoever. I originally opened Fantasyland to be a bookstore. We were selling comic books, baseball cards and a lot of that sort of stuff. It just gradually morphed into a record store when we started selling a few records. Then it came to a point where records were the only things anybody wanted to buy. So we got rid of everything else and concentrated on vinyl. That was many years before CDs started coming out around 1987.

MARK: U2's *The Joshua Tree* was one of the first really big titles that we started selling on CD. That and some really bad Beatles reissues that had come out. They were just horrible quality, but they were out there, and people were buying them up and saying, "Oh man, these sound great!…I think."

CHAD: I'm pretty sure the first CDs that I bought were Depeche Mode's *Violator* and Fishbone's *The Reality of My Surroundings*. I bought them at a mall record store. Before that I bought cassette tapes and some records. When I was a kid, I inherited an old stereo from my parents that had a turntable and an 8-Track player. I remember listening to George Carlin's *Class Clown* on 8-Track. Then I started buying records that I read about in skateboarding magazines—Misfits, D.I., GBH, Suicidal Tendencies—and I started playing them on the record player. I was absorbing '70s and '80s culture at the onset of the early '90s!

MARK: Yes, I grew up near Tucker. Kind of over near the DeKalb County–Tucker area. I started out here as a customer. Back then, I was into buying records by the Beatles, Beach Boys. I still am. I was into a lot of Athens bands, like R.E.M., and North Carolina bands, like Let's Active. Indie bands...the Smiths, the Cure.

CHAD: You have kept the store open since 1976. By the time this book comes out, you'll be close to celebrating fifty years in business. What have you learned over all these years?

ANDY: There have been a lot of hits and a lot of misses. We've been doing it by the seat of our pants, really, since day one.

MARK: We know what we're doing, though, and it's mostly positive. It's pretty much like any job. If you do it long enough, it becomes sort of like riding a bike. You deal with some crazy people from time to time, but every store has those, not just record stores. There's a lot to learn before you can do it successfully. A lot of people think it's a really easy job, but it can be very stressful.

We've had some people over the years whom we've hired as part-time employees. They worked one or two days and then left after that. They think they're just gonna be hanging out, listening to music all day long, talking to people about music. It is a fun job, but there's always lots to do. Lots of menial work.

CHAD: I worked at a record store in the early '90s, and one of the first and most difficult things I learned was that I had to keep my taste out of it. I would be in the store, cleaning jewel cases and listening to music that I thought was incredible, transcendent. And someone would come to the counter and ask for the lamest thing you can imagine. Enter Jack Black's character from the movie *High Fidelity*.

ANDY: Yeah, and the first thing you've gotta do is put aside your own personal preferences when it comes to music. Just forget all that. You gotta concentrate on what the customer likes and what they're looking for, not what you like.

MARK: Yeah, and we're never rude to anybody, and we never talk down to anybody who walks in the door, or else it would feel like a scene from that movie [laughs]. Everybody has different tastes, and everybody likes different things.

CHAD: I have made the observation that, in the current era, it seems like the era of the cultural stereotype of the know-it-all behind the record store counter is pretty much a thing of the past.

MARK: Pretty much, yeah. You can't stay in business for very long if you treat your customers that way.

CHAD: Also, if you're walking into a record store in this era, you are here for a reason. You're seasoned. You're not a passive shopper.

MARK: Right! They could've gone anywhere else; they could be in a video game store or something like that. But they chose us. They chose to go shopping in a record store, and we want people like that, no matter what type of music they're into.

It's so easy to lose customers these days. People's interests change, and there are so many convenient options now. They could be doing anything, but we have them in here.

CHAD: How has being located in Buckhead—a bit of a drive from Little Five Points, where Wax'n'Facts, Criminal Records and Moods Music are located—affected the store's personality and the growth?

ANDY: Well, I think we're in a much better location out here. This is an affluent area.

MARK: ...But a lot of the east Atlanta and a Little Five Points crowd are of the mindset that they wouldn't be caught dead in Buckhead. It is a little further away. To some people, it probably feels like we're on the other side of the world, especially when you're in your twenties, and Little Five Points is your neighborhood. But we do have plenty of customers who come here that don't seem to mind—they'll come here from Little Five Points or go there right after they leave here. I don't think we've ever had any trouble with people not wanting to come here because it's in Buckhead.

CHAD: Does the location influence the music that you keep in stock?

MARK: No. We've never taken that into consideration. We get so many people from out of state and out of the country stopping by the store. People from all over the metro area drive over here because this is their destination. It doesn't have anything to do with Buckhead.

ANDY: It's basically the same all over the city or all over the state or all over the world, really.

CHAD: What is the biggest seller here at the store?

MARK: Probably classic rock, but I'd say that indie and '80s alternative are close behind. The Cure and the Smiths are big sellers. Young kids are still discovering their music just like they are with the Beatles and the Stones.

The Beatles butcher cover of *Yesterday and Today*, photographed by Robert Whitaker for the album's 1966 release.

CHAD: I've watched your Facebook page, and I've noticed that you get a lot more copies of the Beatles "butcher cover" of the *Yesterday and Today* LP—more than any other shop in town.

MARK: It's weird. We went for ten to fifteen years without getting a single copy in here, and then we got three in a row! Just pop, pop, pop, one after another. You never know what's gonna walk through the door.

CHAD: I've heard that a lot of celebrities have been spotted shopping at Fantasyland over the years. From locals such as Fred Schneider of the B-52s, Chris Robinson of the Black Crowes and Mike Mills and Peter Buck of R.E.M., to internationally known artists including Robert Plant, Eric Clapton, Michael Jackson, Elvis Costello, Mitch Easter, Billy Corgan and even Burt Reynolds. Can you share some stories with me about your interactions with some of them?

MARK: Peter Buck used to come in the store quite often back in the '80s and '90s. I remember the first time, in 1985, I just happened to be playing their latest record, *Fables of the Reconstruction*, when he came in. I can still remember the look on his face. That look of "Cool, they're playing our record!" They were still a "college radio" band at the time. Nice guy.

Robert Plant was on tour in the early '90s when he stopped in the store. He was playing at the Fox Theatre. He was about as cool as you would imagine. He looked just like the "1971 Robert Plant"—jeans, T-shirt, vest and beads around his neck.

The band was traveling in a large tour bus. Except for Plant. He had purchased an early '70s Buick Skylark convertible out in Texas and was following the bus in it! Of course, the car had an 8-Track player in it, so someone must have told him where he could probably find some tapes for it. He bought about twenty 8-Tracks. He then went down to Fleming's, bought an alligator belt...then stopped into Fellini's for a slice of pizza! It was one of those days you never forget!

Michael Jackson was interesting, as you can imagine. A big black limo pulled up outside the store. A couple minutes later, the limo driver came in. Silently walked around the store for a couple minutes, then left. A few minutes later, he returns, this time with a couple of guys behind him. A very short guy, who I recognized as Emmanuel Lewis, and after him, a masked gentleman in a fedora hat. Yep, it was him. They shopped around in the store for about thirty minutes. Michael was very nice and pleasant. Soft-spoken. Bought a large amount of records (yes, quite a few Beatles). Emmanuel never said a word. And then they were off!

4

THE SECRET HISTORY OF CRIMINAL RECORDS

A CONVERSATION WITH ERIC LEVIN

I n August 1991, when he was just twenty years old, Eric Levin moved to Atlanta and opened Criminal Records in Little Five Points. "Man, there were so many failures during those first few years," Levin offered with a mixture of humility and amazement. "Money was impossible, I was living in the back of the store; we were broken into several times. It was all just a really intense time."

Despite the elements working against him, forging ahead as an independent businessman, selling CDs, cassettes, vinyl records, comic books and toys was his one true vocation.

Along the way, Levin founded the Alliance of Independent Media Stores (AIMS) and the Coalition of Independent Music Stores (CIMS), and he is *one* of the founders of the international phenomenon that has come to be known as Record Store Day.

As a business owner, he has survived the tides of changing musical trends and the pressures of physical media competing with online music streaming services. He also suffered a devastating heart attack. Still, he soldiers on, and after more than thirty years, Criminal Records stands tall as Atlanta's most recognizable record store brand. It's literally the biggest record shop in town. We spent an afternoon talking about it all.

CHAD RADFORD: You have been in the record store business since 1984. How did this all begin for you?

Criminal Records in 2012. *Courtesy of Eric Levin.*

ERIC LEVIN: I started out working for a mom-and-pop shop—it's still there—called Atlantic Sounds in Daytona Beach, Florida. I got the job when I was just thirteen years old. Atlantic Sounds was a neighborhood record shop. I can't visualize the distance, but it was just a couple of miles from my house; I rode my bike there every day. I remember the first time I went in there: I saw a Police picture disc badge and I was amazed. I had only read about it in magazines and in books and in the group's discography.

It was the "Don't Stand So Close To Me" picture disc, and I was just kind of in awe over it. I think I was at a diner with my parents or something. It was a beach town, and we were just having a family dinner. I went outside when I was done and they were still doing their thing. So I walked down to Atlantic Sounds, and I bought the picture disc. I don't know why I had twenty-five bucks as a thirteen-year-old, but I did. And I must have been excited or a little out of place as a young kid there. When I got home, I realized that the guy behind the counter had given me the wrong change back.

So I called him up, and I said, "I don't know if you remember me, but you gave me five extra bucks and I'd like to come down and give you the money, but I don't know if I can get back there for a few days." He remembered me. The guy was cool, and when I went back in, I bought something else and I gave him the five. He asked me, not if I wanted a job, but, "What are you doing for the next few hours?" He got me sweeping and cleaning, and just like that, I started working there. I did that all through high school.

CHAD: So you stayed there and became the record store guy?

ERIC: Yeah! Although, at the time, I had no idea of knowing that this was going to be my future. I was the store's afternoon guy—the closing guy. The owner would come in and open up the store around 9:00 a.m., and I would show up after school around 2:30 p.m., until my senior year when I got work release, or work experience, and I was able to leave school at noon. This was a great little record store, and it was a great time to be working there. MTV

Spring Break came to town every year, and 1985 through 1987 was kind of the height of it. Being behind the counter at the local record store was a pretty hip place to be.

CHAD: What kind of music were you into at the time?

ERIC: I was into new wave, DC hardcore, skater-type stuff, but I was also into the nerdy side of things. I liked Simple Minds, and I liked Echo and the Bunnymen an awful lot. That always turned me on way more than the heavy stuff. I was never much of an Iron Maiden fan and never much of a Black Sabbath fan. We sold all of that music in the store, but I was really into synthesizers, and I wore my heart on my sleeve with that stuff.

Criminal Records owner Eric Levin. *Courtesy of Eric Levin.*

CHAD: I imagine that getting a job there when you were thirteen or fourteen years old, and kind of grew up there, you were the record store guy that people went to see and talk to. You probably had a good rapport with a lot of the regulars.

ERIC: I did have a following. The owner played things like the Allman Brothers, the Beatles and the Kinks, so I got to cut my teeth on all of that music. But I was who you talked to if you didn't want that—if you wanted something a little more of the times.

CHAD: You were the guy to go see if you wanted to buy the new Love and Rockets LP when it came out.

ERIC: And that's a perfect example. It took the owner a long time before he gave me any editorial control over the store, but there were fewer releases coming out on "new-release Tuesdays" back then. So he would stumble upon some cool shit that I would discover after it arrived. But then from my reading every magazine from *Maximum Rock 'n' Roll* and the *Trouser Press* to pretty much anything I could get my hands on, I would help him make sense of the cooler stuff that came in.

CHAD: What was the appeal of working there and reading all of these magazines and building up a strong rapport with your customers?

ERIC: I was a musician at the time. I played bass. I played in my high school's jazz band, and I played music with my brother, mostly. He was a drummer, and I was just trying to keep up with him, playing music, listening to music and collecting records. But I was also keeping up with

Big-time industrial music guys! Eric Levin (*left*) in the original Criminal Records. *Courtesy of Eric Levin.*

my father, who had a really big record collection. He had a lot of jazz and avant-garde stuff. With my brother, I definitely followed in his footsteps with new wave and punk. I was definitely getting turned on prior to having the record store gig.

CHAD: Your father was an independent business owner as well?

ERIC: Yeah, he was an optician, and he had his own optical shop there in town.

CHAD: How did you end up in Atlanta?

ERIC: Ultimately, I had a falling out with the owner of Atlantic Sounds, and to be delicate about it…the nicest way to put it is that it was too redneck for me. It was to the point where I thought, "I have to break away from this environment and open up my own shop." I mean…we're talking about a person who would—and probably still does—reenact Civil War battles, but only for one side, if you catch my drift. I just had to get out of there, so when I was nineteen years old, I opened up my own record store in Daytona and called it Secret Service.

CHAD: Correct me if I am wrong, but that name got you into some trouble. Is there a law that says you are not allowed to name a business Secret Service?

ERIC: Yep, there sure is. When they enacted the Secret Service, this was just an arcane, way deep-in-the-books law with the notion that if somebody was trying call to help save the life of the president—if his life was in danger—they didn't want people to have to go through a further step to get to where they needed to go if they're trying to get in touch with the actual Secret Service.

For some reason, I have no idea why, I called my store Secret Service Records. I ran it by my lawyer, my CPA, I put the name in the newspaper for six weeks, I registered it with the state and did everything you're supposed to do. I made my signs, T-shirts, business cards, all of that stuff. I started out with just a teeny, tiny little shop in Ormond Beach, which is adjacent to Daytona. That's my hometown. This would have been 1989. I had the place up and running for about three or four months when two agents came in. I actually wasn't in the shop at the time; I had just walked across the street to get a Slurpee or something from the convenience store. When I came back, there was one dude with a black-and-white suit and another dude with a Hawaiian shirt. It just felt like a scene from *Lethal Weapon*—they were totally the typical movie characters. They took me in the back and explained the situation to me, and then I was arrested.

CHAD: They put you in cuffs?

ERIC: Yep! I was later released on my own recognizance. Everybody knew that this was a total bullshit charge, but I did have to go down for processing.

When I got out, my lawyer said, "Change the name immediately. Whatever you do, do not fuck with these guys! Let's get this over with and behind you." He was basically telling me to shut up. And I would've followed his advice, but there had been a reporter for the local paper in the store, and he took the story and ran with it. So by the time I got out of the court, it was a news story, and there were cameras everywhere. It was front-page news in the area. A television reporter was doing a story and at the end of his broadcast, he quipped, "Well what's he gonna call the store now, Criminal Records?"

That was it! The next day we were Criminal Records. All these years later, it's a pain-in-the-ass name. It always has been. It's a dumb joke. We get lots of phone calls from around the country: calls from sheriff's looking for information. When we were a little snottier back in the day, we would just say, "No, we're a record store, man!" But now, let's just help people get to where they need to go. We've received lots of weird mail over the years, too.

CHAD: How long did Criminal Records last in Florida?

ERIC: Like a year and a half at the most. It really was a rash decision when I opened it. It was a rash decision when I changed the name. And it was a rash decision when I moved to Atlanta. My brother Corey was moving.

I wanted a weekend off, and he was moving to Atlanta, so we arrived simultaneously. I was sad that he was moving; I loved him and his dog. All of my friends had gone off to college, and I was starting to think, "Man, I'm going to be like one of those guys at the end of the bar who never left. I need to get out of here!"

I followed him up here just to see what Atlanta was like. I think they had just announced the Olympics, and I didn't know anything else about the city, aside from the Atlanta Braves and TBS. And I had a friend who was going to school over at Agnes Scott, so I wanted to see her. So I just drove up and came to Little Five Points.

I had never seen anything like it, and it was so different. I had come from a really culturally bankrupt city. It was fun for spring break, and then it was awful. I distinctly remember arriving before my brother, and I didn't have the keys to his apartment. So I didn't really have anywhere to stay except my car. So I went to Fellini's Pizza at 2:00 a.m. In Daytona, nothing stays open past 10:00 p.m. So I'm in this awesome place; there's killer pizza, cool-looking people, and they were playing Sonic Youth. I had never heard Sonic Youth's music being played outside of my car or my headphones. So to hear that music in public was kinda crazy awesome. So if I didn't decide that night, I decided the next day to make the move up to Atlanta. I started looking around town for "for rent" signs and realtors. The next weekend I drove up again. After having been in touch with a realtor, I found the first location down by the Variety Playhouse, where Java Lords is now. That would have been 1991. I think the store was there for three years.

Then we moved up to the location next to Junkman's Daughter. That was a project of Pam Majors, who is no longer with us. She owned Junkman's Daughter and Don Bender, who owns a lot of property in Little Five Points. Their plan was to refurbish an old grocery store—Value Foods. I had made friends with the Aurora Coffee folks, who were opening up their second location, and we agreed to take 30 percent of their space. That was lean times, but with the help of the landlords we got into that space by hook or by crook in '94.

The Olympics hadn't happened, but they were fixing to. It was gearing up. And when it was over, it was over. Everybody left, the streets were empty, and everybody was just kind of shell-shocked, waiting for what was coming next. Everybody was figuring out what to do with all this new stuff on a city level and all of these new people.

CHAD: Did you notice an increase in people coming into the store and buying music after the Olympics?

ERIC: The increase was drastic when moving from the small location to the big location—it's kind of hard to think of it as big now, but things picked up when we moved that year.

On a personal level, my life was really just getting started. I got married, got a home and got that location filled. I have never been a terribly good businessman—not then, and not now. But at that time, my strategy was to just take the money, buy the stuff, put whatever's left in the bank, take the

Top: Urban Urbane: David J of Bauhaus and Love and Rockets signing Records at Criminal Records' Euclid Avenue location in the early '90s. *Courtesy of Eric Levin.*

Middle: Crack the Skye: Brann Dailor (drums) and Brent Hinds of Mastodon (guitar) during a Criminal Records in-store performance in 2009. *Photo by Robin Henson.*

Bottom: Spiritualized performing a live acoustic version of "Lord, Let It Rain On Me" in the parking lot in front of Criminal Records' Moreland Avenue location in 2003. *Photo taken from a live video shot by Video Raheem.*

money, buy the stuff. It was grueling and fun, and so much happened there. We were doing such major in-stores on a constant basis.

CHAD: I remember seeing Kool Keith, Krist Novoselic, Lou Barlow, Bill Callahan, Danzig, Spiritualized, the Jurassic 5, the Polyphonic Spree, Deerhunter, Black Lips, the Coathangers, Mastodon, all in that location that's now Stratosphere Skateboards.

ERIC: Yes, there were several Mastodon shows out there in the parking lot in front of the store. Weezer was a pretty big one in that location. Andrew W.K. came to the store and worked for a day—he sold records and chatted up customers. He remains so cool to this day, but at that time your jaw just had to drop. He was like the Keanu Reeves of rock stars. I remember his tour manager was giving him a hard time and was saying, "Dude, you're late for sound check, you've got to leave now!" He was so nice to every single person, but he turned to his tour manager and said, "Don't tell me when I leave. I'm doing this."

He was on the phone leaving voice messages for people, telling them the CDs they ordered had come in. And it's like, Andrew, you should go and take care of what you have to do! What a cool guy.

CHAD: What was the first in-store you ever booked?

ERIC: You won't believe this, because I know you're a fan of the time period. In the Florida store, we booked A Split Second. They were totally Belgian, and I don't even know if they knew what an in-store was, but the store was so small and so dumb, and they just arrived and played, and it was awesome.

The first in-store I ever had at the first Criminal store here in Atlanta was Mary's Danish. That was amazing. We also did an in-store with Lush, which was the first open event when we moved to the location next to Aurora Coffee. They were in the store, and they just walked over and played at the Point.

In the current location we recently did Mumford and Sons and got three hundred people in the store for that. We did the Raconteurs; Ride recently played in the store. There was one day when we did an in-store with Indigo Girls, and then the store cleared out and Mastodon came in and played a set.

A reporter once wrote that Pearl Jam did an in-store at Criminal Records, and I remember Sean at Wax'n'Facts got mad about it. He was like, "They did not do an in-store there!" But the group *did* hang out in the store for an afternoon. They just showed up. They were in town, we had a Sony branch here and the Sony guy was my roommate at the time. He brought them to

Top: Amanda Palmer during a Dresden Dolls in-store performance at Criminal Records. *Photo by Kathryn Pollnac.*

Bottom: The Meat Puppets performing live in 1994, in front of Criminal Records' first Little Five Points location. *Courtesy of Criminal Records.*

the store and was like, "What am I gonna do with these guys? We could go to lunch, we could go to the record store?"

They just ended up hanging out and playing basketball at the school across the street, which is so Pearl Jam. I was smoking weed with Stone Gossard in the back—I think it was Stone....Maybe it was Matt. Or was it the drummer who got fired? Anyway, Evan Dando and Juliana Hatfield played a huge in-store for us. That was probably my biggest crowd to date. That was when the store was in the small location, so that would have been 1992. That was one of my earlier ones.

I did a David J in-store in 1993. It was an RCA event. It was the day after my brother died. He missed the in-store. Max Eider was playing accordion, and it was totally amazing. It was a big one for me, as a huge fan. All the in-stores before that were great events. I like Evan Dando, but David J was the first one where I was like, "Whoa."

In the summer of 1994, the Meat Puppets were in the process of scoring an honest-to-goodness alternative rock hit song with "Backwater." The group was passing through town as a daytime act on the H.O.R.D.E. Tour. After their set, they made their way to Little Five Points to play an in-store at Criminal.

It was at the original location. The band set up in front of the store to play on the sidewalk, as the hillside across the street filled up with people who'd come to watch. The crowd steadily grew. For real, hundreds of people were there. It wasn't that the Meat Puppets were a big draw; it was just a beautiful sun-shiny, breezy day, the band sounded amazing and the crowd just grew and grew....Oh, and there was some really great acid going around the neighborhood, too.

The band had played just a few songs when a police cruiser came down Euclid Avenue and slowed to a halt, between the band and everyone who'd flocked there to hear the music. I thought, "Oh, great, they're going to shut us down, and I'm going to get a fine for this." But the cop lingered there for just a few moments; he surveyed the crowd, looked at the band, nodded his head and slowly drove away. The people who'd gathered on the hillside roared with applause, and the band took it as a cue to rock out even harder.

I knew then and there that somehow everything was going to be alright

CHAD: I will never forget the Glenn Danzig in-store circa 1999 or 2000. I was new in town, and I'd found a job working next door to Criminal Records at Junkman's Daughter. I took my lunch break to go get the new Danzig CD with the limited-edition artwork signed. People were saying, "Don't bring any Misfits records, 'cause he'll get pissed off!" But when I got in line, he was signing tons of Misfits, Samhain and Danzig stuff. I even saw one guy getting the *Less Than Zero* soundtrack signed. Todd Youth was there; Joey Castillo was there. It was a Samhain and Danzig tour—for *Danzig 6:66: Satan's Child*.

He came to Junkman's after the signing. He had an assistant with him, named Scum. I helped them with a clock that was designed by an artist called Richard Ramirez. We talked about action figures and things like that. Glenn told me how much he hates the movie *Scream*. I had a coworker who introduced herself and told him that she played in an all-lady Misfits cover band, called the Miss Fits. He seemed genuinely stoked to hear that and asked about what songs they play, who sings, all kinds of stuff. He was supremely cool. I also remember watching Danzig draw a skull on the windowsill at Criminal.

ERIC: I still have all the windowsills and all the walls that people wrote on. They're in the attic at the new location. If you'll recall, a lot of the in-stores that happened at that shop were before cellphones…definitely before cellphones had cameras, and unless someone shared photos with me, I didn't capture a lot of the in-stores that happened there over the years.

CHAD: When did you move Criminal Records to 1154 Euclid Avenue?

ERIC: The first Record Store Day was celebrated in the shop when it was over by Aurora Coffee in 2008. You did a DJ set that day. The Coathangers played. Janelle Monáe played outside. Andy Hull from Manchester Orchestra played inside. That was a great send off to the old store. We moved soon after that.

All of the Record Store Days have been great up until the last three years. They're still great, but they haven't been great live events. It's become so much harder to do live events, whether it's the promoter war, Atlanta traffic or lack of label support. We still try as hard as we always have to get good events, and we have had some *really* good ones.

CHAD: Criminal is still the strongest brand in town when it comes to record stores. You've had layoffs and raised your prices. Criticism has died off over the last decade, but there was a public backlash to the "Save Criminal Records" initiative in 2011, when you asked the public to help save the store from drowning in debt and unpaid taxes. Still, when people think of Atlanta record stores, they think Criminal Records. That's a hard-earned brand. Does it feel to you like Criminal still plays the same role in people's lives?

ERIC: It's a multifaceted question. We definitely don't have the cachet of a Grimey's in Nashville or an Amoeba in LA. I can take as much of the blame as possible for a downturn. But there are also lots of things to hang it on: the rise of streaming music, the dominance of Amazon, the plethora of other great record stores in Atlanta. Not that there's not a ton of competition in a city like Austin, say for Waterloo or for End Of An Ear. They've got dozens of specialty record stores. Indianapolis has Luna, and that's like an iconic, precious record store. There's Shake It in Cincinnati, which is one of my favorites, but in the past five years he's had so many stores open up there. If you're getting in your car and you're running around in a big town, you can't visit them all.

We've come off a dollar high to a manageable and appropriate level. We're certainly looking for growth. Years ago, there was a mania for record store culture that's not there anymore. But a lot of what we have seen return has to do with the resurgence of vinyl. A lot of vinyl-only stores have popped up. Some of them are awesome. They have style, and they concentrate on used records.…Will they all be here five years from now?

Maybe they'll be here, and the big legacy stores won't. Or the opposite. It's difficult to speculate about the future. We've gotten so expensive. I look through the bins, and I say to myself, "Oh my god, really?"

CHAD: I lived through the '90s and was even buying records in the late '80s. I've experienced just about everything that the archetypal record store dick trope could level at me. Today, it seems like people who work at record stores are so dedicated to keeping the store open that they actively engage you, because it's such a vocational role for them. Is the era of the Jack Black/ *High Fidelity* record store dick over?

ERIC: Under my current regime—and it's exactly what you described— my crew is as nice as possible. Until I hear something. And then I'm like, "You said what? You did what?"

Recently, somebody harshed us online about not letting their kid go to the bathroom. And it's like, well…I don't have enough staff. It's a giant place. It takes somebody off the floor to let a kid go to the bathroom. I need those eyes on the floor. It's not set up for kids to go to the bathroom. The employees are empowered to take care of the customer, but there are signs that say, "No bathroom," you know? But on the other hand, just let the kid go to the bathroom!

The comment they left on Google is lengthy: this is against the law and I'm gonna do this, and I'm going to do that. It's an upset mom. But go to any restaurant in the neighborhood. You read these comments and start to feel angry about it and want to respond. But at the same time, any record store customer is going to read that review and say, "Huh, they didn't let a kid use the bathroom…Whatever, do you have any This Heat records?"

But multiply that by a thousand little cuts.

You are right about the dick thing. Amoeba Records: For years, I have always asked out loud, "How does Amoeba train everyone from the door guy to the poor kid I'm making climb way up high on a ladder to be on the same level?" Everyone there is totally nice. Amoeba has always been amazing.

CHAD: What's next for you?

ERIC: Everybody thinks about it, except I've never thought about it. I have a hard time thinking about it, particularly after suffering through a heart attack a few years ago.

What am I capable of now? What interests me? What would I do? I think about it late at night, and I don't have any answers. I would be foolish to think that Criminal Records has another decade in it. But maybe it does. It's not something I envision. What are we as a species going to look like in ten years, let alone this little record store? It's not a dark time outside of

Top: Goodie Mob signing copies of *Age Against the Machine* at Criminal Records circa 2013. *Courtesy Criminal Records.*

Middle: Puddles Pity Party at Criminal Records in 2015. *Courtesy of Eric Levin.*

Bottom: Mick Jones of the Clash, Big Audio Dynamite and Carbon/Silicon (*left*) for a Criminal Records in-store signing in 2008. *Courtesy of Eric Levin.*

what we've talked about, which by the time your book comes out, won't be a factor because of distribution issues. We will still have a bunch of used records and a trickling of new records.

I personally don't have children. I'm not having children. I've got a very small house. I'm not gunning for a new car, so the store doesn't have to do much more than what it is already doing—existing, trying different things and employing people, which is cool. Sometimes those daily totals are like, "Whoa! I haven't seen that since the early days!" But at the same time vinyl is still doing wonderfully. There's always a house call to go buy some greased up, dirty records. Or hey, here's a stack of audio file records! And they're coming through the door every day. They all take a lot of time to scrub and take care of the pricing. There's a lot of work to be done. I could potentially see Criminal shrinking because it's in such a big space, but it's also comfortable. But, you know, the landlord could change the script on me.

You know, maybe people wouldn't assume that I think this way, but someone like Danny Beard at Wax'n'Facts is a hero. He's a trailblazer with everything from his record label, DB Records, to having been in this neighborhood since '76. That's awesome. That's amazing.

CHAD: Outside of Criminal Records, what else do you do?

ERIC: I am the president of AIMS, and that is the Alliance of Independent Media Stores, which is an organization I started. We primarily sell advertisements, price and positioning of new releases.

CHAD: My perception of AIMS is that…say Amazon or Barnes & Noble or some other big box store all have massive buying power and get stock at a lower price than independent stores, because the indie shops can't order as much as the big box stores. AIMS helps indies get that volume discount.

ERIC: That's part of the benefit of our advertising. The advertising guarantees a buy-in and sale price and positioning, social media posting. It makes things easier for the shrinking music industry. They've fired all of their salespeople. Okay, so I am a salesperson for thirty stores. And our counterparts CIMS, the Coalition of Independent Music Stores, have 45 stores. Then there's the Department of Record Stores who have, I believe, 110 stores. Bull Moose up north has 7 stores. They have Zia in Arizona which has 14 stores. So together we act politically. We created Record Store Day, and we run that. So that's actually been a lot of what my time has shifted toward. For the most part, when a label is putting out a record, they include our programs in their budgets.

CHAD: One of the things you hear often around here is that Eric Levin created Record Store Day. Can you clarify how it was born?

ERIC: It's amazing that a true story can be looked at from so many different direct angles. Years ago, we had an event called Noise In the Basement, in Baltimore, and we were sitting around, just a small group of us—the three presidents, two of our right hands—in a couple of other stores. It wasn't a very big group. We met in the lobby of a hotel and were sitting around asking, "What are we going to do? What can we do to look out for the future?" And this is where I come in. I said, "Why don't we do what we did with Free Comic Book Day?"

In reality, everything was going really well at that time. But all of the journalists, and all the articles we were reading, were leaning the other way, saying these guys are dinosaurs. These guys aren't happening. So it was like, what do you mean we're not happening? We'll show you how happening we really are by throwing parties at each store.

My notion was free music, let's get the labels to give us free CD samplers and free things. After an hour of talking, we all thought, yeah, let's do this! Let's get back to our home base and all work on this. So we quickly ramped up and did it that first year.

Now, Chris Brown from Bull Moose says he created it because he told his president, Michael Kurtz, at the Department of Record Stores....And that's because we all said, when you get back to the store, make this part of your discussion. Let's have a party at the record stores. Michael Kurtz might think he started it because he came up with "record store day." Don van Cleave, who was part of CIMS at the time, might think he started it because he was there in the beginning, so the truth is, yeah, I started it, but with a lot of other people.

CHAD: It sounds like a lot of people had their antenna dialed into the same frequency, and you were one of them.

ERIC: I just brought my expertise as a participant. Newbury Comics was in that meeting as well, and their representative thought it was a terrible idea. I said, "Well, you do Free Comic Book Day." Her reply was something like, "We just put a box of free comics on the end of the counter." I said, "If that's the case, you're doing it wrong." So in some ways she was a creator as well.

CHAD: There will always be those who despise Record Store Day. I'm sure you hear the phrase as much as I do: "Every day is Record Store Day," and this annual Hallmark-style holiday uses manufactured scarcity to line up a bunch of tourists and posers with their wallets out.

ERIC: I see the online threads, and I see the emails and the comments… [even] the international comments. I also see the ones from shop owners

T Bone Burnett taking it all in at Criminal Records, back in the '90s. *Courtesy of Eric Levin.*

saying that they would have thrown in the towel by now if it weren't for Record Store Day.

I listened to the labels, and people have said, "My job was in danger, but I'm billing so much now." For a twice-a-year event—which I was never a huge fan of Black Friday—our job is to get people into the stores and to buy stuff. I have never liked the idea of lesser products, and even though it's nothing I envisioned, because I wanted free stuff, Record Store Day grew based on market demands, and the demand is still there.

When I hear customers worldwide saying that they feel a certain release is unnecessary, I urge them not to purchase it. But yes, every day is Record Store Day. We're open 363 days per year. I am somewhat immune to that criticism. I am also part of the team that vets the releases.

There are multiple times a day where somebody says, "We're gonna release a certain record" that I personally don't give a fuck about, so I'll say don't release that one! One year, there were four Tony Joe White records being offered to us for Black Friday. It ain't my thing, *but* I bet Grimey's would do really well with them, so…I do the same things that the people on the internet are writing: "*The Coneheads* soundtrack? What the fuck? Who needs that?"

CHAD: Who needs the *Emmet Otter's Jug-Band Christmas* soundtrack?

ERIC: Dude, I said that we weren't making nearly enough of those! That was one of my favorite HBO kid shows. It's awesome. I love that shit and knew it was going to be a sellout.

A more apropos example might be *Baby Shark*, which is a total kids' song. As I have said, I don't have kids, but even I knew that that song was hitting the zeitgeist.

It's like a two-year-old song, and it was coming out on really pretty blue vinyl, with a T-shirt and a stuffed shark. I knew that we wouldn't be able to order enough of them. I was telling the AIMS stores to order thirty of them, order sixty of them if you can afford them. And it was the instant sellout of the day. Any mom with a carriage, and I mean every parent who walked back there bought one.

A few years ago, Billie Eilish put out a white-label 7-inch. Nobody had heard of Billie Eilish at the time. I just took the time to look it up, and thought, "Oh, this is something," and I brought in five copies....We could have sold twenty. Imagine what it would be like now!

5

ELLA GURU RECORDS

I've always said that the only way to sell records is over the counter.
—Don Radcliffe

In the interest of full disclosure, I work at Ella Guru Records from time to time. I'm one of the fill-in guys who gets called whenever someone is sick or needs to leave town. I can always plan on spending any money that I make there on records, because everything that you've heard, the tall tales of mind-blowing records lining the walls and the bins at Ella Guru, is true.

It's all used vinyl. Owner Don Radcliffe runs a tight ship, and he knows the value of a well-curated selection. Be it Mobile Fidelity Labs, hip-hop and electronic dance music 12 inches, classic or obscure rock nuggets, country gold, serious jazz scores or deep cuts from Marion Brown, John Coltrane, or Sun Ra, Radcliffe's dedication to quality over quantity is what keeps his lifelong customers coming back for more.

CHAD RADFORD: Whenever I travel to a new city, and I visit new record stores, it feels like the Ella Guru model is kind of a new standard. The store is clean, used vinyl is the chief product, and the people are helpful. The paradigm of the snooty record store guy seems to be a thing of the past.

DON RADCLIFF: Frankly, you have to have something to feel superior about, and if you're super young, that's not a big group of records out there. If you're super old, you can feel superior about all kinds of stuff, but there just ain't enough guys out there to give somebody the attitude.

Left: The famed three-dollar bins along Ella Guru Records' storefront circa 2020. *Photo by Chad Radford.*

Below: Ella Guru Records coming soon to Oak Grove Plaza on Lavista Road circa 1999. *Courtesy of Don Radcliffe.*

Opposite: Ella Guru Records: Hanging up the sign in 1999. *Courtesy of Don Radcliffe.*

Dude, I recently bought two Liza Minnelli Mo-Fi records. Somebody's gonna come walking in the store and will want to buy it, I hope....But I bought it in the first place. I ain't no smarter than anyone else.

CHAD: How long has Ella Guru been open?

DON: We've been open here in the current location since November of 2012. But we opened the CD store in '99. It first opened up in the strip where the Subway is now. There used to be a soul food place called Quinnies. We moved into that space. Never clean out an old restaurant. When we pulled the plastic off the kitchen walls, it was like a scene from that movie *The Mummy*. Roaches just completely covered the wall. That was in the first place in '99.

In early '02, there was a popular neighborhood grocery store called Ned's IGA that anchored the location. They closed. The landlord was super nice. Then I moved over to Toco Hills, and we hung in there for another seven years. That was when I started selling new stuff. But it was a lot more fun when I was selling nothing but used records with low rent.

Then I was in Inman Park for only six months. The scooter guy who was next door wasn't paying his rent. He went chapter 7. Belly up. He wasn't restructuring or nothing. He went from printing money at Paris on Ponce to the whole thing blowing up. The famous second location problem. It never fails. If you can make it through location two, you're going to do fine. But most people don't make it through the second location.

Especially if it's goodwill. If you're not there, it's a different deal. I would have loved to have hung in there. Just imagine what the next four years would have looked like. Old Fourth Ward blew the hell up!

Of all of the gentrified, BeltLine things, Old Fourth Ward is the most unbelievable. I worked at one-stops back in the '80s. If these guys would have known what would happen with neighborhoods like Kirkwood and Oakhurst, they would have said, "That's where we used to buy smack!" I wouldn't buy a house there, but we used to buy heroin there.

When we moved out of Old Fourth Ward, it was like being in the wilderness. What kind of job does somebody who's been in the record business their whole life get?

There was a three-year gap. I did a lot of odd jobs, sold stuff online, it wasn't pretty, but my wife has a pretty good job. She's self-employed. We hung in there. Whatever part-time shift I could rustle up, I'm a guy in his fifties who knows a lot about records. I applied for a job as the manager of the FYE in Douglasville. They didn't even call back. I have thirty-some years in the biz. Would you at least like to talk?

CHAD: How did you find the store's current space?

DON: The short version of the story is: Melissa and I, and our baby, Ella, used to go to Evan's Fine Foods on North Decatur Road and Clermont every Saturday and eat pancakes. We watched families grow up there. We went from that to watching Ella realize that it was much more fun to sleep in on Saturdays than it was to go eat pancakes.

The family that owned this strip mall—Pete, the owner's son, said, "We'll put you back in business one of these days. We've got a tenant that makes a lot of noise. One of these days they'll be out of here and you'll be in here to start up the store again."

CHAD: What was here before?

DON: Before Ella Guru, this was a little hair salon, called Bee-Hive. Before that it was something else. And before that, there was a guy who is still probably wondering why he was fifteen years ahead of his time. He sold beer-making supplies. This guy was here in the '90s and was way ahead of the curve on making beer.

When we made the decision to open the CD shop, the idea was low overhead, high markup. I'd have banquet tables and cardboard boxes in here if I had to, but Melissa won't have it.

CHAD: Let's talk about the shop's dynamics.

DON: We strictly sell used records. Basically, this is sort of a late '70s, early '80s record store. We're missing a lot of stuff, but as long as there are decent records on the shelves, with a good markup, we'll keep going. Doing low volume with high markup is easier than doing a business plan, figuring out your budget and basically selling stuff with a 25 percent margin. That's what you have to do with new records, and what we had to do with CDs when we moved to Toco Hills. We knocked down a wall, doubled the size of the place, and I thought an ad in the paper was gonna be what we needed.

The one hundred dollars they paid to put a light box of an album cover in the window every month was a drop in the bucket compared to the capitalization costs. By the time we moved over there, the writing was already on the wall.

During that time, stores were vanishing left and right. Any chain that existed back then is now gone. Tower hung in there until the bitter end. There was Media Play. But now they are all gone. We sort of regretted our decision, but said, "Go big or go home!" And we hung in there, but it was really tough.

Recently, I had one of those blue Parlophone Beatles box sets in the store. I sold it to a guy who said, "What I really need is a red one!"

The red one is a mono box set, pressed in '83, I think. They pressed four thousand copies of the set. Two thousand of them were sold in the UK. The other two thousand were sold exclusively at Turtles. That's a lot of juice! In the '80s, Peaches closed down, and Oz closed down, and Record Bar was a mall thing. Turtles, on the other hand, was on damn near every street corner in the city. They were a major force.

I knew a lot of guys who worked there. I eventually went to work for Doug Wiley at Important Records, which became Red. We ran it from the back of Wax'n'Facts. Me and him, two phones and a fax machine.

We were selling indies and imports to record stores. Wiley did mostly Record Bar. He did business with the home office, and he also sold directly to the record stores. And it was like, "Act now, because we just got seventy of these things in!"

When a Depeche Mode 12 inch came out, Record Rack in Houston and Oaklawn in Dallas would order sixty copies of these records, have them overnighted, and they'd sell them all that weekend and never order them again. If it wasn't a club banger, nobody's gonna want it.

Douglas hired me because Important had signed a deal with Megaforce. They would be doing a lot more business with the Metallica record that was just coming out, and then there was Megadeth and Slayer up next.

CHAD: This whole side of the business has been totally dismantled.

Adding up the numbers: Ella Guru Records owner Don Radcliffe in front of Ella Guru's 2747 Lavista Road. location in Decatur circa 2018. *Photo by Chad Radford.*

DON: There is nothing about this business that is the way it used to be, really except for this, running a small independent store.

I see Josh Feigert doing it on a much smaller level with his State Laughter distro and online store. I know he goes to a lot of punk and hardcore shows and sells records there, too. He's selling to people, not to stores. I don't know if anyone is buying imports and putting them under one roof and calling up indie stores.

The main reason is because records aren't returnable. It's 100 percent of the reason why you don't have indie distributors selling imports. Heck, it was thirty years ago, but we would take them back, and we would gripe like a motherfucker. But if big accounts wanted to return stuff, we'd give them a return authorization, and then New York would sit on them forever and not give them credit.

That's just how it works. If you don't take returns, why sell records?

The Scorpio catalogue was like the new phonebook is here. The minute the Scorpio catalogue came out, every retailer in America was checking things off, and trying to order in real time. There's only so many of them that would be cut out.

Don Radcliffe (*left*) with Sean Bourne, Harry DeMille, John and Sarah Byrd and Alice DeMille at Wax'n'Facts circa 1988. *Courtesy of Don Radcliffe.*

If the record didn't sell, they sent the stuff to a cut-out company, and that was all she wrote. They would sell for cheap at other mall record shops.

Important needed a salesperson in Austin. The mid-'80s was a good time to be there, but my gig slowed down.

CHAD: So why do it?

DON: It's just my savant thing. I've been around these things for so long, I am fairly confident that I know what to buy. And I've always said that the only way to sell records is over the counter.

I'm comfortable here. You get to know the guys who come in, and it's a great feeling to be able to hold out a record when they walk in and know that they want it, before they even say anything.

When you carry used records, you notice patterns. I'll pay more for recent stuff, and I'm seeing more and more of that, from the year 2010 and forward. I also think there are a few people who are culling the herd, and for them, it doesn't feel wrong to pay twenty dollars for a record and then sell them for five.

I read this thing a long time ago that said, "Music is liquid now. You cannot hold it. It will go where it needs to go. It will seek its level and if you put an impediment in front of it, it will go around it." Of course, that's exactly what happened to it. That part of what's been happening is incredible.

> *Honestly, I think that Ella Guru is the only record store in town where my record would actually sell.*
> —*Atlanta Braves organist Matthew Kaminski*

On game days at Truist Park, home to the Atlanta Braves, organ player Matthew Kaminski can be heard laying down grooves from the press box. "Green Onions," "Good Vibrations" and, of course, "Take Me Out to the Ball Game" are just a few of the go-to melodic chords that he plays when star pitcher "Maximus" Fried, outfielder Ronald Acuña Jr. and the rest of the team takes the field.

In November 2021, Kaminski self-released his first vinyl offering, titled L.A. Connection. The album finds Kaminski teaming up with drummer Jeff Hamilton and guitar player Bruce Forman on seven cuts of spacious and swinging West Coast jazz tunes, covering everything from the Beach Boys' "Help Me, Rhonda" to the George Braith–penned "Boop Bop Bing Bash," given a classic, organ trio makeover. There's even one original song on the album, titled "Macuba."

When not plucking out game day ambiance for the Braves, Kaminski can also be found playing University of Georgia baseball games in Athens, performing with the salsa band Orquesta MaCuba and teaching music to students around the world via Zoom. Somehow, he also finds time to scour through local record stores, searching for rare organ jazz and Beach Boys LPs.

When it came time to find an outlet to sell his own record, Ella Guru Records, lying at the cusp of Decatur's Leafmore, Oak Grove and Sagamore Hills neighborhood, was the obvious choice.

Atlanta Braves organist Matthew Kaminski. *Photo by Emily Butler Photography.*

MATTHEW KAMINSKI: Ella Guru is the *only* record store in Atlanta where I have my record, *L.A. Connection*, for sale. There is one record store in Virginia Beach, of all places, called Birdland Music that carries it as well. Whenever I go to visit my in-laws who live up there, I make it a point to stop by the shop—the owner of the store actually asked me to send him some records, so I did.

I met Ella Guru's owner Don Radcliffe at the store at some point. Ella Guru is one of those shops where I would just hop in and out from time to time. Don was always so nice. I don't know if it's like this for other people, but when I am in a record store, I don't want to talk to people. The reason why is because I'm concentrating on what I need to buy. It's not like I'm antisocial or anything like that. I'm on a mission, concentrating on what I already have at home, what I want and what I need.

Honestly, I think that Ella Guru is the only record store in town where my record would actually sell. I go to a lot of other shops pretty often: Decatur CD, Wax'n'Facts, Wuxtry. Those are all great places, where I find stuff on a regular basis. I have taken some of my things into a few other shops, and I don't think they'll ever leave the shelves. But I know that with Ella Guru, Don has it right there on the wall with a bunch of really cool records, and he'll talk it up to people, if he thinks it might be their thing.

Ella Guru is the only shop in town that I go into and start talking to the people behind the counter, because I've gotten to know them. It's just really easy to strike up a conversation. Don had once mentioned to me that he's a baseball fan, which is probably how me playing organ for the Braves came up in our conversation.

Quickly, I came to realize that Don possesses a really broad knowledge of a lot of different kinds of music. It's just as easy to talk with him about baseball as it is to talk with him about jazz or the Beach Boys. So we had a connection.

Occasionally, I will get Instagram or Facebook messages from him saying, "OK, we have this Jimmy McGriff album in the store right now. Do you have this one? Do you need it?" I think he's holding a couple of things for me behind the counter now. And Don is the kind of guy who will hold on to something for three months—till I have to go in and ask if he's holding anything for me.

The main things I am always on the look for are jazz organ records. I'll go ahead and say that I'm a fanatic when it comes to finding obscure Jimmy Smith or Jack McDuff records. It's what I do as a musician. There are plenty of other things I look for, of course, like Beach Boys stuff, which I already have all of it. But then I'll go in there and find things like the *Spring* LP. I think in Europe they call it *American Spring*. But it's an album that was produced by Brian Wilson—he sings on it and plays various instruments—with his wife, Marilyn Rovell Wilson, and his stepsister whose name is Diane Rovell. Anyway, it's Brian Wilson in 1972, which is kind of a rare era for him, and the record is a really rare thing. I had never seen it out in the wild before, until I found it at Ella Guru. That's probably the rarest thing I've been looking for and found there.

The cover art for Matthew Kaminski's *LA Connection* LP released in 2021 by Fairfax & 3rd. *Courtesy of Fairfax & 3rd.*

So, I'm always searching for those albums that are related to the Beach Boys. Sometimes I'll be on the lookout for polka records, too. I play accordion in a polka band, called the Georgia Polka Connection. Sometimes I'll look for salsa records, but I'm mainly on the hunt for jazz and especially jazz organ records.

I also play a lot of what some people call Gypsy-style jazz, which is like Django Reinhardt–style jazz. So, naturally, I'm looking out for a lot of those kinds of things as well—Django Reinhardt and Stéphane Grappelli records. In Europe, it's more of a prominent thing to hear an accordion on jazz records. There was one guy who played with Django quite a lot, named Gus Viseur. He's kind of thought of as the Django Reinhardt of the accordion.

Sometimes I'll find the best stuff in the three-dollar bins that Don has in the crates outside, in front of the shop. I have found baseball organ records from the 1950s or the '60s in there, or like a Denny McLain record. There is a lot of variety in the store, even in those cheap record bins outside.

6

DISORDER VINYL

On October 16, 2021, just when it felt as though there would be no end to the ongoing COVID-19 pandemic, Yoonsang Doo established himself as an Atlanta record store lifer. At the young age of just twenty-seven, Yoon opened Disorder Vinyl, a new record shop tucked inside an unassuming warehouse at the corner of Ormond and Fraser Streets in the burgeoning Summerhill neighborhood.

This new venture expanded Yoon's already deep forays into the business of serving DIY and underground music. In 2013, he launched Floodlight Records, a hardcore record label that went on to release several 12 inches and EPs by bands such as Houston's Narrow Head, Savannah's Coastlines (later dubbed Vatican) and South Florida's Prayer Chain.

Yoon was a fan of alternative rock while growing up. But when he discovered hardcore music and culture as an early teenager amid Jacksonville, Florida's small but bustling scene of the mid-aughts, his tastes, and his ambitions to be a part of the local community, came into focus.

His background has much to do with the mostly new vinyl LPs, 7-inch singles, cassette tapes, CDs, books, zine, and T-shirts that fill up what has quickly become Atlanta's most dynamic specialty record shop. When LA's rising hardcore outfit Militarie Gun traveled the country supporting their All Roads Lead to the Gun II *EP, Yoon pushed the racks aside and made room for the group's only Atlanta show.*

And when the legendary Circle Jerks' bass player, former Joe Strummer cohort and Kevin the nerd from Repoman *Zander Schloss ducked out of the Masquerade between sound check and showtime to hand-deliver copies of his solo album,* Song About Songs, *to local record stores, Disorder Vinyl was priority one.*

The shop's versatility extends beyond its selection of spectacular hardcore LPs. Disorder is also the exclusive retailer for many local and regional hardcore, post-punk

Disorder Vinyl circa 2020. *Courtesy of Yoonsang Doo.*

and alternative rock releases. The in-house label even pressed up the self-titled 12-inch EP by local act Hubble, blasting four songs that blend equal parts post-hardcore and atmospheric shoegaze textures into fractured and self-conscious melodies and guitar attacks. More releases are on the way.

Before closing up the shop one quiet and sweltering evening in July, Yoon took a few minutes to talk about his ongoing quest to dig deeper into music and to offer some insight into what makes him tick.

CHAD RADFORD: Let's start by talking about the name of the shop: Disorder Vinyl. How did you choose the name?

YOONSANG DOO: One thing about me is that I hate naming things...with a passion.

The idea of naming a project, a song, my cat or anything at all is super daunting to me. It's a permanent thing. Once it's put out into the world, you have to roll with it, and there are very few things that I have named in the past, or that I've been part of, that I'm especially proud of. Even previous bands that I've been in, I'm just like, "Oh, this name sucks!"

The idea for Disorder was in my head for a while, but the name didn't materialize until May or June of 2021. That's when I needed to set up the LLCs and the licensing, and I needed to have a name. So one day I was listening to music, and as many have probably guessed, I was rocking Joy Division's *Unknown Pleasures*. The first track on the album is called "Disorder," and I thought, "That could be a cool name for a record store."

It's short, to the point, and it has a punk edge to it because the word is a little jarring. A few of my friends said that it's a funny name for a record store, because people might expect to walk in and find this place in a state of total disarray. But I never thought of it like that.

CHAD: I've never thought of it like that either. It makes me think about having a mental disorder, i.e. buying too many records, or like these records can take the edge off of whatever your disorder may be…something like that.

YOON: Exactly. So, then I thought: "Disorder Records?" I really didn't want to use the word *records* because it feels too obvious. But "Disorder Vinyl" rolls off the tongue, and you can shorten it to just "Disorder." So, I went for it.…And here I am!

In the past, I've had a handful of record labels. I was fresh out of high school—seventeen or eighteen years old—when I started my first label, Floodlight Records. I wanted to do a label purely because I wanted to contribute to the underground music scene in Jacksonville. I used student loans—my Pell grant—to pay for my first record, and I have no idea why I chose to name it Floodlight Records.

After that, I did a project with my roommate, friend and bandmate Kaleb Purdue. We started Fruit Stand Press, which was designed to be more than just a label, but a place for all kinds of creative outlets. It was short-lived. We only did one release, Slow Fire Pistol's *Beauty* 12-inch EP.

After that, I was going to do another label by myself, but I never got around to it. Then I was gonna start a label with a guy in Boston.…Never got around to that either. Then Disorder Vinyl opened up, and now I release things in-house, like the Hubble 12 inch.

To this day, the two records that I did with Narrow Head are my only two releases that have done well—and by "done well" I mean they broke even. It's a labor of love for me. Losing money is no fun, but I don't mind too much. I just want to see the projects that I put my energy into come to light, which is really all that matters to me.

CHAD: How did you make the shift from running your own label to running a physical record shop?

YOON: A big push for me was COVID. I lost my job, and I had been around to help a buddy of mine, James Siboni, open up Tiger Records in Jacksonville. I was around while he was doing it, and I watched him do really well at it, which encouraged me to say, "Okay, I want to do this too!"

Disorder Vinyl owner Yoonsang Doo, running the shop. *Photo by Chad Radford.*

I thought, "If I can't find a job, I'm gonna make a job." I've been wheeling and dealing records, T-shirts and music paraphernalia for much of my life. So, I decided to do this more seriously, and create a space, which was my main goal. Anyone can sell records through Discogs or eBay or whatever. But brick and mortar is so important in this day and age. Everything is moving further and further away from analog. Just the thought of flipping through record bins and putting more effort into seeking out music is way more fulfilling than looking at your Spotify related artists.

CHAD: Was there one record store that left an impression on you while you were growing up?

YOON: Jacksonville is not a major city like Orlando or Miami, but it has some things to offer. Unfortunately, it didn't have much of an alternative scene when I was growing up. We had a small hardcore, DIY and punk scene, which was cool. There were some record shops in town, but they didn't really carry much of what I wanted.

There was one shop in Gainesville, called Arrow's Aim, which was like an hour and thirty minutes away. The owner was named Daniel Halal. He's still in the music business but just online these days. He's a genius when it comes to music; he just knows so much. It was always a pleasure going there, because I could always find something—the most niche things ever—that made me say, "Wow, this looks cool! I'm buying this!" That was the regular store. I first went there in 2013 when I was nineteen years old. I got my first car when I was eighteen and was actually able to go places on my own.

CHAD: When did hardcore come into the picture for you?

YOON: My first hardcore show was in January 2010. I gravitated toward alternative music while I was growing up. I actually took my older cousin's Linkin Park CD, *Hybrid Theory*, and was listening to it and thinking, "Oh my God, I don't know what this is, but it's awesome!" I didn't know what heavy, aggressive music was, and here's this guy who's just screaming. That's cool! And I guess that's what started it all.

I started listening back when rock was more of mainstream music and was hearing things like Green Days, Blink 182. I was listening to a lot of that and watching music videos on Fuse, etc. When I was in middle school, I wanted to play in a band. So, me and my friends started this pop punk band back in like eighth or ninth grade, called Fight for First.

When the band started, I was really just interested in being part of the local scene. There was a local band called Set the Record Straight, who were playing a show at a venue called the Pit in Jacksonville. I was like, "Let's go!" So, me and my friend, who was the singer of our band, drove in his car over to the show. It's just the two of us, and he just leaves me there! He's like, "Dude, I have to go take care of this stuff with my girlfriend," or something like that. I said, "Dude, you're just gonna leave me here?"

I was this tiny wimp in a venue full of scary strangers. And he says, "Dude, I'm so sorry," and he left!

So, I'm there by myself. I'm like fourteen or fifteen years old, and I paid my ten dollars or whatever, which, as a teenager scraping by, was the equivalent of one hundred dollars, and I realized the one band that I went to see was packing up. I'm like, "Oh God, they already played!"

But at the time, I was stoked to support whatever I could support, so I was like, "Oh, well I guess I'm stuck here." I was trying to watch every single band, and I'm mesmerized because the place was going nuts! People were jumping off the stage! Controlled violence. Mosh pit stuff.

The lineup had Down to Nothing, Kids Like Us, Trapped Under Ice, Cruel Hand, Naysayer, Forfeit, I think this band called Harbinger from south Florida played, xTyrantx....I think Set the Record Straight was the opener. It was a mini fest in Jacksonville, and as it turns out, a lot of my friends I've met while traveling to other cities in Florida for shows were all there at the same time! We just didn't know each other yet.

That was my introduction to hardcore. The craziest, coolest thing I had ever experienced. There was so much adrenaline, so much good energy, and one band that I remembered was Cruel Hand. Upon getting home, I looked them up on Myspace and saw Have Heart, Shipwreck, Guns Up, all of that in their top eight. It all just kind of rolled from there.

For me, Myspace was the first digital version of something like liner notes and thank-you lists that I had seen. When I started finding music, it was during the tail end of the CD era. I would get a CD and read everything that was in the booklet, but I was definitely on the ground floor of the digital age of finding "related artists" via Myspace's top eight.

It was cool because it was curated to what the bands themselves fucked with, like, "We are Cruel Hand, and we support *these* bands." Cool! I like *this* band, and they like these bands. I will probably like these bands too. It started a chain reaction. I saw this band's top eight, and then another band's top eight, and I was just absorbing as much as I could get from there.

CHAD: Instant gratification like that is a much different experience from the tactile relationship you have with music that comes stamped onto a piece of physical media, though.

YOON: The instant gratification of something like Spotify's related artists has its benefits, but it has more drawbacks. In a scientific way that I can't really explain, it ruins our attention spans and creates a throwaway mentality, where we don't give the music time to sink in. We're just like, "Oh, this sucks. Next!" The first vinyl record I ever got was Foundation.

CHAD: The Atlanta hardcore band?

YOON: Yeah! I saw them on a tour in 2011, and they had a copy of their LP that just came out, *When the Smoke Clears*. They were the first hardcore band that I super gravitated toward. They're still one of my favorite hardcore bands. Still number one.

When I first saw the vinyl record on their merch table, I thought, "Oh, this is cool!" I had such an outsider perspective with this record that I thought was just a cool tchotchke for this band that I love. Kind of like how random people will have Michael Jackson's *Thriller* hanging up on their wall for whatever reasons. It was kind of like that for me with the Foundation. I thought, "I love this band. This is a cool novelty to have."

It was a gatefold, and upon opening it, I found all of this cool artwork, there were inserts, hidden liner notes and just so much more information that I could not find online. I had an iPod, and I had downloaded all of the music already. But this was something different altogether.

This brought a whole new dimension to the music. Vinyl is an art form in and of itself. There's so much more effort that goes into the packaging and everything else. I fell in love with it, and I thought, "I want to collect records by every great band that I'm into!" I've spent a lot of my time and money and effort on it ever since.

CHAD: There's also something very pleasing about the ritual of putting a record on the turntable, putting the needle down and just waiting for the sound to physically fill the space between the speakers....And you're not staring at a screen.

YOON: It goes hand in hand with the experience. I can put something on Spotify right now and just play anything at the tip of my fingers, but it takes even just that little ten seconds of extra effort of putting on a record and walking away, which reinforces your brain to care and to appreciate the music for what it is, and love it, rather than reacting after the first ten seconds and throwing it away.

CHAD: What have you learned from owning and running Disorder Vinyl?

YOON: I have learned that I know nothing about music. There's this running joke with my friends and I about how I know very little about pop culture. Like, terribly little. I know a decent amount about some things, but my friends will be talking about a movie scene, and I'll say, "I don't know what that is." And they're all like amazed: "You didn't watch this?"

Funny example, but I have still never watched *A Clockwork Orange*. I don't know actors, actresses, and I do not know some very seminal bands. This is gonna sound so blasphemous, but I had never listened to a full Beatles record until I opened the store.

CHAD: How did that happen?

YOON: When I was growing up, classic rock never appealed to me. One, I had immigrant parents who didn't know about it. They listen to gospel and classical music. I didn't have a dad or a mom that listened to Lynyrd Skynyrd or Led Zeppelin or whatever the hell else you want to say. My music taste was formed when I got help from my cousins.

Generally speaking, growing up in the 2000s, I listened to what I thought was cool at the time. When I was little, I thought Metallica sucked. I thought it was garbage, dad rock! Over time, though, I realized that it actually rocks.

I'm listening to a lot of the classics for the first time, which is hilarious and kind of blasphemous, being that I am a record store owner.

CHAD: There's no shame in that. As someone who worked as a professional music journalist for more than two decades and has bought records obsessively since Ronald Reagan was president, I have found that there is always another truly great, classic record to be discovered. That's what keeps me going back into record stores!

There is no end to the number of records that people hail as milestones of culture—the deeper you go, there will always be a jazz artist, a punk 7 inch, a hip-hop CD that has somehow escaped me 'til now.

Also, I have zero interest in pop culture on the surface. Top 40 music, mainstream music is just in the way of truly good music. The banality of popular music is what forced me to start digging deeper. Of course, my perspective on that is always changing to a degree, but I am more interested in pop culture's outliers.

YOON: I think pop culture is important, but when I was growing up, I never gravitated toward it. I could give a shit about what the hell the Beatles did or didn't do. I liked Nirvana's songs, kind of, but I didn't gravitate toward that kind of stuff until I gained a deeper appreciation for music. It just never occurred to me to give a shit.

CHAD: But at some point, you did start giving a shit.

YOON: Oh yeah! The more nerdy and mature I got, I just wanted to know more, and dove deeper and deeper into music history.

A lot of people listen to music at face value. If you're living in the year 2022, and you're a young kid or teenager, and you hear something from the '70s for the first time, you're probably thinking, "This kind of sucks."

But if you put yourself into the position of, say Ozzy Osborne in the '70s, writing a song like "Paranoid," you realize that it was a crazy time in the world, especially in the UK. A lot of things that influenced that period of writing and that specific record. That is fascinating, and it has a lot to do with the product that was created. Music is subjective, and that's what is beautiful about it. Anyone and everyone has a different viewpoint. No one is right or wrong.

CHAD: Have you developed a strong rapport with a lot of your customers?

YOON: Yeah. I have a good group of regulars who I see weekly sometimes. Some people come in every two weeks. I can kind of sense their tastes now. If it's a top-tier customer, I can generally say, "Hey, I have this in the store. I didn't put it out yet." You might be interested, and nine times out of ten, they'll want it, unless they already have it.

I have developed a nice relationship with a lot of my regulars but with new customers, too. Honestly, people that I meet for the first time, I like to ask how they found out about the store. That's good marketing insight that lets me know what's working. Remembering peoples' names and faces and getting to know them helps me suggest other things for them.

If they come in here, I want them to be able to learn about new music. That's the cool thing about record stores. While you're flipping through the bins aimlessly, you might see something that you used to really love, and you're reminded of that.

When people come in here for the first time when they're on dates or with their BFFs or whatever, they're just like, "Dude, remember this record? We used to listen to this all the time!" Good times, good memories come out.

Sometimes if you see certain artwork that's really cool you think, "I might like this a lot!" People will take a chance on something, take it home and learn about something new.

That's something I really like about having the shop. It's nice to see new faces here. Some people come in and sometimes they don't buy anything. That's fine, too. If you're having a good time hanging out with your friends and talking about music, that's the end goal here. The whole purpose of the store is to create a space for people to come together with the shared passion of music.

CHAD: The algorithm can tell you what you might like, but nothing beats a solid human interaction, especially when it's done over music.

YOON: It creates a better human connection. Anyone can buy a record on Discogs or Amazon or whatever. But I like to buy stuff from a brick-and-mortar store, if I can. It's like supporting your local restaurant or hairdresser or anyone that's a real person and not a corporate entity.

CHAD: If you go to Wax'n'Facts, you can buy a B-52s record from the guy who put out the B-52s' first record! You can have a unique experience with the source! Nowhere else can you get that experience. The guy who put out their record is sitting there behind the counter, waiting to have a go at you!

If you come here, you have the Foundation record. You have the Abuse of Power record. You don't see those anywhere else. You have knowledge and a perspective to share that can only be found right here. You can't get that from the internet.

YOON: Honestly, a big reason for this store opening, too, was just purely for the fact that through no fault of anybody, punk and hardcore in record stores is kind of hard to come by, which is crazy ironic. Punk and hardcore were literally the lifeblood of vinyl records for decades!

There was a time when vinyl records were not cool, when CDs were coming out. Every major label ditched vinyl because CDs were more profitable and easier to make. The only people that were still producing records were in the underground scene, mostly hardcore and punk kids. So it's crazy ironic that punk and hardcore are the least present things in a lot of record stores. There isn't a specialty shop for that kind of stuff in Atlanta, which is what I wanted to provide for the underground.

It's funny, on that note, a lot of people that are into faster, punkier, heavier stuff now found out about this music through Tony Hawk's Pro Skater video games.

CHAD: That's an excellent point.

YOON: That's also kind of how I started, because I was into skateboarding, even though I can't skate for shit. I thought the culture was cool. I enjoyed playing the video games, and then you're just playing for hours and like AFI is on repeat, and so are the Ramones, Suicidal Tendencies and some hip-hop stuff. It's just like all on repeat constantly. You fall in love with the music because you associate it with this cool thing that you're doing.

Then all of a sudden you're into fast, aggressive music, and you're like, "Oh, I guess I'm this guy now!" Honestly, that is how I started listening to a lot of music, granted it was on a very surface level. But you've gotta start somewhere.

7

WISE WORDS FROM CLIFF KRAPP

I met Cliff Krapp in June 1999. I had just moved to Atlanta after graduating from the University of Iowa, and I was on a mission to scope out every record store that I could find. After scouring through the yellow pages, using the now long-antiquated phonebook like a checklist, I made my way out to Eatmore Records. The shop was located in an unassuming blue cinderblock building on Jimmy Carter Boulevard—not too far from where Netherworld Haunted House was located for years, before relocating to Stone Mountain.

I walked in, and the place was a clutter of boxes stacked on boxes leaning every which way. Each one filled with 7 inches, LPs, CD and tapes. It was somebody's organized mess. There was order to the chaos, but it eluded me. The white-bearded and bespectacled man hanging out behind the counter offered a hearty greeting and asked if I needed help finding anything.

"No, thanks," I replied. "I'm just looking around."

He persisted. "Well, if you do think of something that you're looking for, just let me know."

"All right, I said. "I am looking for something by a local group, called the Rock*A*Teens."

I had caught them playing a live show at Gabe's Oasis in Iowa City, less than a year before I moved to Atlanta. At the show, I had gone to the merch table and picked up what was, at the time, their brand-new album Baby, A Little Rain Must Fall, *on Merge Records. It was fantastic. Songs with titles such as "Teen Muscle/Teen Hustle," "I Could Just Have Died" and "Ether Sunday" conjured a noisy and melancholy sonic haze of reverb-drenched heartbreak. This was the shadowy, sweet and broken sound of the South that I had moved here to find—music made by outsiders living*

Cliff Krapp (*left*)
and Bella Reece at
Wax'n'Facts for Record
Store Day 2019. *Photo by
Chad Radford.*

among outsiders: the Beach Boys' Pet Sounds, *the Ramones'* Rocket to Russia, *Joy Division, Jan and Dean, William Faulkner, Walker Percy, Cabbagetown.*

On the drive to the store, I heard a pair of WREK DJs interviewing singer, guitar player and the group's principal songwriter Chris Lopez. It was the universe speaking to me through the radio.

I asked about the Rock*A*Teens, and without missing a beat, he navigated the maze of boxes with varying twists and turns, He reached a shelf that was hidden somewhere behind a tall stack of even more boxes that were packed so full of records that cardboard was bursting at the edges, and he pulled back two CDs: The Rock*A*Teens 1996 self-titled debut, and their '97 CD, titled Cry, *both released by Amy Ray's Daemon Records. Both sported the same crystal clear and haunting imagery of photographer Chris Verene.*

"Anything else you're looking for?" he asked.

"How about some Misfits, Samhain or Danzig albums?"

He leaned way over to another hidden enclave of the store and produced a sealed copy of Danzig IV on cassette. The only one I hadn't ever listened to at the time. I coveted it.

Our interaction went on like this for a while. Clearly, he was some sort of record store wizard. I didn't introduce myself until we crossed paths again, when Eatmore moved to its final and more distant location on Sugarloaf Parkway in Lawrenceville. When I walked through the door, our interactions were the same. "Do you have anything by Sebadoh?" He hustled to the racks and returned with copies of Smash Your Head

On the Punk Rock, Bakesale, *and a handful of CD singles—"Flame," "It's All You," "Ocean" and the almighty "Rebound."*

We made small talk. His kindness was striking then as much as it is now. Cliff was a much different record store guy than many of the Jack Black circa High Fidelity*-type characters that I had encountered during my time in the Midwest. The South was still a new thing for me, but engaging with Cliff at Eatmore went far beyond the tropes of southern hospitality.*

CLIFF KRAPP: I've had people come up to me and say, "You recommended this to me years ago, and I still love Spiritualized, or I still love Verve, or you found that weird Oingo Boingo record that I just couldn't track down anywhere else!"

When you've worked someplace for twenty-four years, you get to a point where you meet people's children, and they come up and say, "My dad used to bring me in....I remember you from back then!" Then you get to know *them*, and that's cool.

CHAD RADFORD: Where does your instinct come from when it comes to engaging with others about music?

CLIFF: Let's not go overboard here—I am by no means a saint. When you're into something, anything, you are too cool for school, at least for a while. If you're into baseball, you know all the statistics, but if your friends aren't into baseball, you're just like, "Well, I know my shit!"

I've been working at record stores since I was fifteen years old. I went through that phase: the Cure and Echo & the Bunnymen? Yes! Hall & Oates? No!!! That sort of thing, even though I love Hall & Oates. There are so many great bands that I regret not going to see in the '80s, because I was too cool for school.

When I started working for Craig Freireich at Eatmore, he was a little older than me. People need to have someone who's older and who can teach them what they're not going to learn about in books. When I was sixteen, I didn't know or understand the importance of someone like David Bowie, for example. You have to learn it from somewhere, and you have to have someone play you some stuff to find out if you like it or not.

When I first came to town, I found Turtles Records. I came from Columbia, South Carolina, which still is a hillbilly wasteland. I was like, oh my god, imports of Madness! Imports of bands that I love! I'd never been around anything like that at all!

So, when I moved to town, I opened the phone book, and started going to every record store that I could find. One day I went to the Book

A sign from the original Eat More Records. *Courtesy of Cliff Krapp.*

Nook, and I was buying something. I don't remember what it was. David T. Lindsey was working there, and he started talking to me about what I was buying. I said that I didn't really know much about it, and he asked me what else I was into. I told him about a few things. He asked, "Do you have any Stooges records? You need a Stooges record in your life." I didn't know who that was. He asked if I knew of Iggy Pop? Of course I did. He said it was Iggy's first band, so I went and got a copy of *Raw Power*, and I fell in love with the Stooges. And that's why I fell in love with being in record stores.

When I started working for Craig, '50s and '60s nostalgia was hitting big. It wasn't dealing with just Cure, Siouxsie and Bauhaus records. I was talking with older customers, and they were telling me about all of this old shit that they were into. And they were just as geeky as I was about new shit—although most of them turned their noses up at Frankie Goes to Hollywood and all of that new wave "crap" that I was into. But I learned a lot from them, and I gained a lot of respect for other music that I wasn't into. At some point, I remember thinking, that anyone who gets out of their car and walks into a record store and wants to buy something is cool.

I didn't care what they were buying, whether I liked it or not. When that movie came out, sometime in the '90s, and the Jack Black character became such a thing, people just loved bringing it up in the store. I hated that! You're not going to get that with me. I give a crap that you came in here and want to talk about music. I don't give a crap that you don't like Echo & the Bunnymen or the Rave-Ups or whatever I was into at the time.

I love looking at people's stuff, too. You want to invite me over to your house so I can look at all of your avant-garde records? Let's do it! I'll sit there for hours looking at them and asking you all kinds of questions about them. I probably don't care about them, but I care that you are so into them that you spent years plundering record stores for these avant-garde records.

Collections of anything interest me. They tell me that you are interesting enough to have a predilection for whatever it is that these things have to offer. It's the idea of being so interested in something, and to take it back to the base level, anyone who gets out of the car and says, "I really like that

Eagles song," or I really like that Einstürzende Neubauten song, or the hip-hop song that I have to sing to you….And then I say, "That's Young MC." That's cool to me, you don't have to know everything about Young MC to comment on my Young MC records.

If you're asking why I was always nice, that's just how I looked at people coming into the store. It was someone who was interested in music. I was there because I was interested in music. What could be bad about that? I don't have to love death metal to talk death metal with you. I just like anybody who's excited to talk about music.

CHAD: When I was fresh out of high school, I worked at Drastic Plastic in Omaha. It was primarily a punk rock, hardcore and indie rock record shop.

I was kind of a dick back then, but I had an ah ha moment: I was deep into industrial music: Coil, Throbbing Gristle, Einstürzende Neubauten, Z'ev, the Legendary Pink Dots…You name it! So I would be working in the store for hours having something akin to a spiritual experience, listening to all of this heavy music, and people would come in and ask for something that seemed ridiculous to me.

One day, this guy walked into the store. He was a big guy; he kinda smelled bad. I was deep in the zone, and he walked up to me and said, "I drove all the way from Kansas City. Do you have anything by a band called Butt Trumpet?"

There was something about this guy asking for Butt Trumpet that made me want to give him a hug. I think that was the moment when I got over myself and realized that nobody cares about how many Can and Philip Glass and Legendary Pink Dots records I have spent all of my money acquiring.

This guy drove all the way from Kansas City, looking for Butt Trumpet. That is admirable. And that is awesome. This was before the internet, and you couldn't just hear music when you wanted to. You had to seek it out, sometimes go on epic journeys to other cities to find it!

Ska was big back then, and in my opinion, you couldn't have committed a bigger party foul than being into ska. But people would come in the shop looking for ska, and I had to suppress these feelings of: *How dare you approach me and ask me about ska?*

Now, I would love nothing more than to have a meaningful conversation with you about the Toasters.

CLIFF: You were having your too cool for school moment. I think it all boils down to a weird way of taking pride in the work that you've done. You have the knowledge. Think about it like if you were a baker, and you just wanted to say to people, "Look at this awesome cake that I made!" But you and I can't say, "Look at this awesome music that I made," because we're professional appreciators of said interest. We did a lot of work, and we did a lot of listening, and we just wanted to say, "I know my shit!" Maybe it was to get some respect or something like that. But once you settle into the fact that you can have a conversation with somebody about Whitney Houston as much as you can about the Toasters, it all kind of evens out.

8

YOUR FIELD GUIDE TO ATLANTA RECORD STORES

BEATLAB
464 Moreland Avenue NE
Atlanta, GA 30307
(404) 524-9060
facebook.com/BeatlabATL

A BOOK NOOK
3073 North Druid Hills Road
Decatur, GA 30033
(404) 448-2166
booknookbookstoredecaturga.com

CD WAREHOUSE
2175 Pleasant Hill Road
Duluth, GA 30096
(770) 623-1552
www.facebook.com/
    cdwarehouseatlanta

CD WAREHOUSE
50 Barrett Parkway # 3025
Marietta, GA 30066
(770) 425-3472
www.facebook.com/pages/CD-
    Warehouse/107880365967261

COMEBACK VINYL
1 South Main Street
Alpharetta, GA 30009
(678) 580-0583
comebackvinyl.com

CRIMINAL RECORDS
1154 Euclid Avenue NE A
Atlanta, GA 30307
(404) 215-9511
criminalatl.com

DBS SOUNDS
6604 GA-85
Riverdale, GA 30274
(770) 997-5776
dbssounds.com

DECATUR CD & VINYL
356 West Ponce de Leon Avenue
Decatur, GA 30030
(404) 371-9090

DEPOT RECORDS
251 Hurricane Shoals Road NW
  Unit F
Lawrenceville, GA 30046
facebook.com/DepotRecords

DISORDER VINYL
55 Ormond Street SE
Atlanta, GA 30315
(404) 820-6520
store.disordervinyl.com

ELLA GURU RECORDS
2747 Lavista Road
Decatur, GA 30033
(404) 883-2413
facebook.com/EllaGuruRecordStore

FANTASYLAND RECORDS
360 Pharr Road NE suite B
Atlanta, GA 30305
(404) 237-3193
fantasylandrecords.com

MOJO VINYL RECORDS
36 Woodstock Street
Roswell, GA 30075
(678) 534-5042
www.facebook.com/MojoVinyl

MOODS MUSIC AND SOUL VILLAGE
1131 Euclid Ave NE
Atlanta, GA 30307
(404) 653-0724
moodsmusic.net

OLD SCHOOL RECORDS
1825 M.L.K. Jr Drive SW Suite 4
Atlanta, GA 30310
(404) 637-4454

RAT ROOM RECORDS (located inside
  Big House Guitars)
2323 Cheshire Bridge Road NE
Atlanta, GA 30324
(404) 254-0223
rat-room-records.mypinnaclecart.
  com

THE RECORD LOFT
749 Moreland Ave Ste C202
Atlanta, GA 30316
(404) 947-2345
therecordloftatl.com

RECORDS GALORE
4148 East Ponce de Leon Avenue
Clarkston, GA 30021
(404) 294-5271

SWEET MELISSA RECORDS
146 South Park Square NE
Marietta, GA 30060
(770) 429-0434
sweetmelissarecords.net

WATERLOO SUNSET RECORDS
New physical location will be
  announced in the near future
waterloosunsetsmyrna.com

WAX'N'FACTS
32 Moreland Avenue NE
Atlanta GA 30307
(404) 525-2275
waxnfacts.com

WUXTRY RECORDS
2096 North Decatur Road
Decatur, GA 30033
(404) 329-0020
wuxtryrecords.com

PRO TIP: If you're still reading this, here's your reward. Atlanta is teeming with antique and vintage markets filled with vendors packing tons of next-level records to be stumbled upon, typically hand-selected to sell from each seller's individual collections—the kind of records that you don't typically encounter out in the wild. Check out Mother Lode at 3429 Covington Highway Suite B in Decatur, Kudzu Antique Market at 2928 East Ponce de Leon Avenue in Decatur and Highland Row Antiques at 628 North Highland Avenue. Tales of incredible scores at each of these markets are legendary, even among the most discerning of collectors.

ABOUT THE AUTHOR

Chad Radford is an Atlanta-based music journalist with twenty years of experience in writing, editing and podcasting. Punk, hardcore, jazz, noise, post-punk, hip-hop, metal, modern composition, drone music and all points in between are where his interests lie. He is the former music editor for *Creative Loafing*, Atlanta, and he is the editor of the Smithsonian Anthology of Hip-Hop and Rap. He is an avid nature lover, and he buys too many records.